SIMPLY FLORIDA...
STRAWBERRIES

Strawberry Recipes from
Strawberry Growers,
Their Families and the Community

*"A special thanks to the
FSGA Women's Committee.
They are
Erin Best, Kristie Gilford, EvaNell Griffin,
Teresa Griffin, DeeDee Grooms,
Tami Ham, Sue Harrell, Becky Hutto, Sandy Lott,
Glenda McNary, and Rose Peacock."*

Copyright © 2000
Cookbooks by Morris Press

Printed in the U.S.A. by

P.O. Box 2110 • Kearney, NE 68848

For information on having your cookb(
our FREE information packet or call Toll-F

D1409837

34491 j   1

STRAWBERRY PRODUCTION IN THE WINTER STRAWBERRY CAPITAL

Chances are good that if you are eating a strawberry during the winter, that berry came from Florida. Each year, over 60 million people come to the Sunshine State to visit, have a good time, and leave heavier at the waistline and lighter in the pocket. As part of an exchange program, we send morsels of sweet sunshine to those left behind in the snow. It is our goal to make winter strawberries beautiful, delicious and readily available. But while it may be easy to find and consume Florida strawberries in your hometown, there is a whole lot of work and planning that goes into making it easy.

Our fields are fallow during the summer, when the rest of the nation's agriculture is busily growing food. The same subtropical climate that brings droves of snowbirds to Florida in the winter, brings us summer monsoons, tropical storms, and enough oppressive steaming humidity to make your socks puddle at your ankles. Before air conditioning and mosquito control programs, the only people who "weathered" Florida summers were dumb, poor or hiding from the law.

Insects and diseases love heat and humidity. They can eat or infect about anything you might want to grow. They are particularly adept at destroying strawberries. Wild strawberries are not native to Florida. We don't grow strawberries in the summer. We don't even try to keep them alive during the summer. We treat strawberries, which are perennials, as annuals. During the summer, we sow a cover crop to reduce weeds and increase organic matter in the soil, and stand back as the jungle of either sorghum Sudan, sesbania or peas take over our fields. In early August, we begin cutting the cover crop, incorporating the organic material into the soil.

After the cover crop becomes part of the soil media, the fields are marked for rows. These rows are typically 48 inches apart, with 13 rows to irrigation lateral. The beds are raised by a piece of equipment called a superbedder, which forms a compact, 8-10 inch table for the plants to reside. The beds are sterilized by a fumigant. A thin film of plastic then covers the beds. At the same time, a drip irrigation tube is placed directly under the plastic, usually in the center of the bed.

These two items of technology have revolutionized strawberry production. The plastic film, called plastic mulch, retains the soil moisture and acts as a barrier against the ever-present pests, diseases and weed seed. The black color inhibits weed seed germination and warms the bed during the cool winter production cycle. The drip tube allows the grower to reduce water usage by a half, and match the nutrient needs of the growing plant with the proper fertilizer quantity and location to maximize productivity with insuring water quality.

About two weeks later, the tractor returns with a hole punch, which provides a precise spacing for the placement of the strawberry plants. Bare root plants are set by hand, every 12-16 inches apart, two rows to a bed. In a time frame between the last of September through the first of November, over 100 million plants are set in this manner. Timing for the setting is dependent upon the variety used, with early varieties, like Selva or Sweet Charlie being planted in early October and Camarosas being planted from mid to late October. The plants are established with liberal water, and the first flat of berries is usually picked at the end of October.

By late December, the strawberry harvest is in full swing. Farm workers will harvest from the same field every 3-4 days, grading and arranging the berries into flats for the wholesale market. The berries are collected at packing sheds in the field, placed on pallets, and driven to a nearby cooler for sale and delivery to market. Because of the perishable nature of strawberries, this process is accelerated. Cooling to 32-43 degrees F takes less than 2 hours.

The trip to the consumer may be as close as down the road, or as far as the other side of the world. Most Florida strawberries are shipped by refrigerated truck throughout the nation. International shipments have become more feasible with new cooling techniques and frequent air flights. This process continues at a frenzied rate throughout the Florida springtime, which begins during the Passover and ends on Easter. By then, growers are ready to turn the market over to more northern climates and prepare the fields for the summer's cover crop. The cycle will begin again with the cutting of the cover crop in August.

FLORIDA'S STRAWBERRY COMMUNITY...

In our neck of the woods, if you play name association games and say "Plant City" you will most likely get a quick and enthusiastic "Strawberries" response. Some say the two were linked in destiny before dirt.

That may be so. Surely the sandy loam soil a league east of Tampa grows the sweetest, most luscious berries ever to pass the palate. Just as surely, the railroad's decision to place a depot in the rural community of Itchapuckasassa, a convenient distance from Mr. Henry Plant's hotel north of Fort Brooke on the lazy Hillsborough River, laid the foundation for a long term bond. The railroad opened up Florida to wealthy northerners to vacation in sunny Florida, just as it opened new markets for Florida produce.

It didn't take long for local strawberry growers to learn that Northern consumers, up to their pasty white eyeballs in snow, would pay a premium for mid-winter Florida strawberries, ice-packed in large wooden crates called ponies. That was more than a century ago, and although the industry has changed dramatically since then, the close relationship between community and commodity has been constant.

One reason the strawberry family has been so close is that the whole community has often been needed to work together to provide the resources necessary to make strawberry farming possible. When a freeze threatened, everyone went to the fields to cover the plants with pine straw or cypress troughs. Virtually everyone without a city job picked strawberries. During the Depression until 1954, Eastern Hillsborough County schools operated during the summer, so the farm family children could help in the fields. These "Strawberry Schools" are a part of this community's lore, and participants still have annual reunions to reminisce and embellish on popular tales of the era.

Over the years, the community has grown and the strawberry industry has modernized. Mr. Henry Plant's railroad was replaced first by the refrigerated tractor-trailer, then also by the air conditioner. Strawberries once consumed primarily in the Northeast, now are a winter treat throughout the world. Farms have gotten larger and mechanized. But in spite of the changes, the Plant City-Dover area is still a Mecca for the sweetest, most luscious strawberries around. Moreover, strawberries remain the commodity that made this community, a family.

Yes, the statistics are impressive. This one county produces about 15 percent of the nation's strawberries and virtually all the berries grown during the winter. The commodity has an impact on our community approaching $200 million. The 16 million flats produced each year, if placed end to end, would extend from Plant City to Seattle and back again. But most impressive is the fact that although production in this strawberry haven has been going strong for over a century, the value of the commodity has more than tripled in the last two decades, and could well double in the next decade. If anything, the community's claim as the "Winter Strawberry Capital of the World" seems stronger. If you make every recipe in this cookbook every year, you will be doing your part to keep it that way!

FLORIDA STRAWBERRY
GROWERS ASSOCIATION

The Florida Strawberry Growers Association (FSGA) was formalized in 1982. It is based in Plant City, Florida also know as the "Winter Strawberry Capital of the World." There are approximately 150 strawberry growers that are members of the Association. The mission for the Florida Strawberry Growers Association is to be "Partners in research, promotion and member/community service."

Research: About one-third, combined resources of FSGA and it's sister organization, the Florida Strawberry Patent Service (FSPS) revenue is targeted for research. Since inception, the Association has made contributions for IFAS research in excess of $1 million dollars.

Promotion: FSGA has been hard at work promoting Florida Strawberries. From television and radio commercials to a promotion with Southwest Airlines, we want everyone to know when Florida Strawberries are in season and promote this delicious fruit that made our community a family.

Member/Community Service: FSGA sponsors made grower functions including the Strawberry Jam, Berry Bash, Agritech Educational Session and Trade Show as well as the Fall Growers Meeting. The growers also believe strongly in giving back to the community and have awarded over $92,000 in scholarships and award approximately 15 scholarships a year. In addition each Valentine's Day, growers donate the profits of ten flats of berries to the Redland Christian Migrant Association with the Straight From the Heart Program.

The Association offers two types of membership. The grower membership and associate membership for individuals or businesses wishing to become more involved with our family of growers. To receive a membership packet, please call the Association office at 813-752-6822 or check out our website at www.straw-berry.org.

WORLD'S LARGEST
STRAWBERRY SHORTCAKE

That's right we did it! On Friday, February 19,1999, the city of Plant City came together to break a world record. Plant City volunteers built the world's largest strawberry shortcake that called for 5,000 lbs of strawberries. The cake was 827 square feet and successfully made it into the Guinness Book of World Record. The previous record was set in Canada at a mere 742 square feet.

Here's the world record winning recipe for the shortcake that will serve 12,000 of your closest friends.

* 7,800 pints of fresh Florida Strawberries
* 300 sheet cakes
* 450 pounds of sugar
* 600 pounds of whipped cream

Florida Strawberry U-Pick Information

There are some strawberry u-pick farms in Florida open during the entire season (December-April). However, most commercial farms do not open their fields to u-pickers until the end of the season which is usually in April (depending on the weather). The best way to find what fields are open is to check your local newspaper's classified section. You can also check out the Florida Strawberry Growers Association website at www.straw-berry.org. The u-pick link will list the farms and addresses that have contacted the Association to let us know they are open for business.

- Dress comfortably. Wear loose fitting clothing. Wear a hat or cap and bring sunscreen.

- Bring your own containers.

- If you plan to spend the day, take ice to keep berries cool.

- Select only firm ripe berries. Be careful not to remove the tops of the berries.

- Make an effort to pick every ripe berry on each plant rather than jumping from plant to plant and row to row. The growers will appreciate your consideration and you will reduce the amount of strawberries that are left sitting in the field.

Did You Know?

- Berry flavor is at its best at room temperature, so remove them from the refrigerator an hour or two before serving.

- To help berries retain flavor, texture and nutrients, avoid washing or removing their caps until you are ready to use.

PLANTING YOUR OWN
FLORIDA STRAWBERRIES

The perennial strawberry plant is treated as an annual in Florida because heat sensitive berry plants cannot survive the long hot summers. Begin preparing your soil in September, plant in October and harvest berries from late December until May.

1. Begin by adding nutrients to the soil, till any grass or organic material and let decompose.
2. Sterilize the soil by wetting the garden and covering with a clear, water resistant water sheet. The soil should be sterile after a few weeks.
3. Next it is time to fertilize. The best way is to provide measured feedings of organic or commercial fertilizer several times throughout the season. Apply less in the beginning of the growing cycle to avoid fertilizer burn and apply more when plants are established and producing blooms.
4. After fertilizing you are ready to purchase your plants. Many retail nurseries carry plants during October for home gardeners.
5. Trim off any dead leaves and soak the roots thoroughly to prevent them from drying out. Dig a hole in the soil large enough to spread out the plant's roots. Place plants with the base of the crown level with the surface of the soil. Do not set too deep. Pack the soil around the roots.
6. As the season progresses, keep your berry plants weeded and cultivated. Lay straw, hay or pine needles around the base of each plant. This helps retain moisture, protects against cold weather, prevents weeds and keeps berries clean.
7. The plants will need almost constant irrigation during the heat of the day. After plants are established you will need to watch for pests and disease and listen to weather reports for news of freezing temperatures.
8. If you have further questions, please contact your local county extension office or master gardener. In Hillsborough County, the number is 813-744-5519.

Growing strawberries in Florida is a rewarding experience for the home gardener. At season's end, you will have delicious fruit and a unique understanding of the hard work and patience involved in commercial strawberry production.

STRAWBERRY NUTRITION &
WEIGHTS AND MEASURES

Fresh strawberries per 4 ounce serving, 1 cup

Calories:	55
Protein	1 gram
Sodium	1 mg.
Potassium	244 mg.
Carbohydrates	12.5 g
Fat	0.7 g

Percentage of USRDA	
Protein	*
Vitamin A	*
Vitamin C	150%
Thiamin	3%
Riboflavin	6%
Calcium	4%
Iron	8%

Contains less than 2% USRDA

Strawberry Weights and Measures

1 basket	=	1 pint
1 pint	=	approximately 3 1/4 cups whole berries
1 pint	=	approximately 2 1/2 cups sliced berries
1 pint	=	approximately 1 2/3 cups pureed berries
1 cup whole berries	=	approximately 1/2 cup pureed berries
1 pint strawberries	=	from 12 large berries to 36 small berries
1 quart whole berries	=	approximately 6 half cup servings
1 flat whole berries	=	8 -9 pints frozen or canned berries
1 pint frozen berries	=	2/3 quart whole berries

STRAWBERRY FACTS AND TRIVIA

Q. How did Strawberries get their name?

A. Most people think strawberries got their name from the common practice of growing berries under straw to protect them from the winter cold and late spring frosts. Others think the name came from the practice of weaving together long stems holding ripe fruit to form "straw" of berries. A few refer to the Old English user of the word "strawn" to indicate the random network of strawberry plants allowed to run.

Q. About the Florida Strawberry Season... When is it? How long is it? How many times do you pick? How many crops do you have in one planting? What is your annual production?

A. We plant in the fall, usually October. We start harvesting in November and continue picking until April. During that time, the plant will put on at least three crops. We may pick the same field as many as 50 plus times. The average harvest in one season is 15,000 quarts per acre but some growers will harvest 25,000 quarts.

Q. Why do strawberry growers plant plants rather than seeds?

A. Every strawberry seed contains different genetic material, the product of a myriad of potential gene combinations. Because the genetics of strawberries is so diverse (humans are diploid, strawberries are octoploid), each of our varieties came from a single seed, which was cloned from a single mother plant. The mother plant puts out runners (called daughter plants) that were essentially identical to her, which in turn also put out runners. Last year, we planted over 40 million plants from one variety, each of which was identical to their great, great, great grandmother found to be a good selection maybe ten years earlier.

Q. In these times of increased water conservation, what are strawberry growers doing to use less water?

A. In the recent past, strawberry growers have voluntarily reduced their water by over a half, through reuse of collected field runoff and drip irrigation. Today 98 percent of Florida's strawberry acreage utilizes drip irrigation. Public supply admits that 12 percent of the water pumped from the aquifer gets lost in the pipes and never makes it to the consumer. There is irony in the fact that public supply loses 3 times as much water from leaky pipes than the entire strawberry industry uses to produce a crop.

TABLE OF CONTENTS

Sips to Savor

Champagne Berry Cocktail, page 5
Chocolate Covered Strawberries, page 106

Punches, smoothies, shakes, coolers, teas and lemonades

SIPS TO SAVOR

FOUR FLOWERS JUICE

FSGA Women's Committee

6 fresh STRAWBERRIES
4 bananas, peeled, cut into
  pieces
2 c. chilled orange juice
½ fresh pineapple, peeled,
  cored, cut into chunks

1 c. cold water
2½ T. pure maple syrup
2 T. grenadine
1 T. fresh lemon juice

Combine bananas and ¼ cup orange juice in processor and purée. Transfer to pitcher. Combine pineapple chunks and ¼ cup orange juice in processor and purée. Transfer to same pitcher. Mix in water, syrup, grenadine, lemon juice and 1½ cups orange juice. (Can be made 6 hours ahead. Chill. Stir well before serving.) Pour fruit mixture into tall glasses. Garnish with strawberries and serve. Makes 6 servings.

STRAWBERRY KIR ROYALE

FSGA Women's Committee

2 c. halved STRAWBERRIES
1 T. sugar
½ c. chilled champagne or
  sparkling wine

1 T. creme de cassis

Mix strawberries and sugar in medium bowl. Let stand 5 minutes, stirring occasionally. Divide between 2 large wine glasses. Pour ¼ cup champagne and ½ tablespoon cassis into each glass. Makes 2 servings.

STRAWBERRY-LEMONADE PUNCH

FSGA Women's Committee

1 pt. sliced STRAWBERRIES
1 (12-oz.) can frozen pink
  lemonade, concentrate
1 (6-oz.) can frozen orange
  juice, concentrate

1 (12-oz.) bottle ginger ale,
  chilled
Vodka (opt.)

Combine lemonade, orange juice, strawberries and 3 cups water in container; refrigerate until ready to use. Pour lemonade mixture into punch bowl; add ginger ale slowly. Add Vodka; stir well.

STRAWBERRY DAIQUIRI

FSGA Women's Committee

1 pt. STRAWBERRIES
1 (6-oz.) can frozen limeade

Light Bacardi rum

Place strawberries and limeade in blender. Fill blender with crushed ice. Pour rum (measured in limeade can) over ice. Blend to desired consistency. For a special dash, add pieces of soft peppermint to mixture before blending ingredients or add 2 tablespoons of creme of coconut for a tropical taste.

ICED STRAWBERRY TEA

Megan Freel

1 pt. fresh STRAWBERRIES
4 c. cold tea
1/3 c. sugar

1/4 c. lemon juice
Ice cubes

Set aside several strawberries for garnish. Purée rest in a blender; strain into a pitcher. Stir in tea, sugar and lemon juice until sugar dissolves. Chill. Serve over ice; garnish with strawberries.

STRAWBERRY RHUBARB FOOL

FSGA Women's Committee

1 pt. fresh STRAWBERRIES,
  halved
3 c. sliced rhubarb
1/3 c. sugar

1/4 c. orange juice
2 c. light whipped topping
Fresh mint, opt.

In a saucepan, combine rhubarb, sugar and orange juice; bring to a boil. Reduce heat; cover and simmer for 6-8 minutes or until rhubarb is tender. Cool slightly. Pour in a blender container; cover and blend until smooth. Chill. Just before serving fold rhubarb mixture into whipped topping until lightly streaked. In 6 chilled parfait glasses; alternate layers of cream mixture and strawberries. Top with strawberries and sprig of mint if desired.

STRAWBERRY SLUSH

Margaret Rodwell

1 (20-oz.) pkg. frozen
  unsweetened STRAWBERRIES,
  thawed
2 (15¼-oz.) cans crushed
  pineapple

3 c. orange juice
Lemon-lime carbonated
  beverage

(continued)

2

In blender container combine half of the strawberries, 1 can of undrained pineapple, and half of the orange juice. Cover; blend till smooth. Pour mixture into ice cube trays. Repeat with remaining strawberries, pineapple, and orange juice; pour into additional ice cube trays. Cover, freeze till solid. At serving time, remove cubes from trays. Place cubes in a large ice bucket or bowl. To serve, place 2 or 3 ice cubes into individual glasses; slowly pour carbonated beverage in glass. Stir gently to make a slush. Serves 30.

FRESH FRUIT PUNCH

Teresa Griffin

1 c. fresh STRAWBERRIES, cut	1 qt. orange juice
½	2 c. pineapple juice
2 c. sugar	2 oranges, washed & sliced with
1 c. fresh pineapple, chopped	peel
1 c. hot tea	1 qt. ginger ale
1 c. fresh lemon juice	Fresh mint for garnish

Dissolve sugar in tea, cool. Add 2 cups sugar, 1 cup hot tea, 1 cup fresh lemon juice, and 1 quart orange juice. Freeze enough of mixture to make block of ice to fit punch or serving bowl. Chill remaining mixture. When ready to serve, pour punch over ice block, stir in fresh fruit and garnish!

DOUBLE-BERRY MILK SHAKE

FSGA Women's Committee

1 pt. fresh STRAWBERRY	¾ c. milk
halves, frozen	¼ c. powdered sugar
1 pt. STRAWBERRY ice cream	½ tsp. vanilla extract
Garnishes: sweetened whipped	
cream, STRAWBERRIES	

Process strawberries, milk, powdered sugar and vanilla extract in a blender until smooth. Add ice cream and process until blended. Garnish if desired.

STRAWBERRY WINE PUNCH

Rose Peacock

2 (10-oz.) pkg. frozen sliced	1 c. pineapple juice, chilled
STRAWBERRIES in syrup	1 (28-oz.) bottle club soda;
½ c. sugar	chilled
1 bottle rose wine	Ice or Ice ring
1 (6-oz.) can frozen lemonade	
concentrate	

(continued)

In a punch bowl, combine strawberries, sugar and 2 cups rose wine. Cover and let stand at room temperature for 1 hour. Before serving punch, add frozen lemonade concentrate and pineapple juice. Slice until lemonade is thawed. Stir in remaining wine and club soda. Add ice or ice ring. For kids, substitute the wine with grape juice.

STRAWBERRY SMOOTHIE

Margaret Rodwell

1 c. fresh STRAWBERRIES, sliced
4 scoops vanilla ice cream

4 ice cubes
½ c. powdered sugar
1½ c. milk

Place all ingredients in blender in order listed. Blend on high until mixture is creamy.

STRAWBERRY LEMONADE

FSGA Women's Committee

6½ c. fresh Florida STRAWBERRIES
3 c. water

1½ c. sugar
½ c. lemon juice

Cook the water and sugar together until sugar dissolves. Cool and chill. To make the lemonade purée the strawberries in a blender or a food processor, combine with the lemon juice and sugar syrup and serve with ice cubes. Yield: 6-8 servings.

STRAWBERRY AMARETTO

FSGA Women's Committee

1 pt. fresh Florida STRAWBERRIES
3-6 T. amaretto

1 pt. vanilla ice cream
12 ice cubes

Combine all ingredients in blender. Blend until smooth. Yield: 6 servings. Frozen strawberries can be substituted for fresh.

STRAWBERRY COOLER

FSGA Women's Committee

1 c. fresh or frozen Florida STRAWBERRIES
1 c. yogurt, plain or vanilla

1 c. milk, whole, skim or 2 %
2 T. honey or sugar

Mix in a blender until smooth and serve. Yield: 3 servings. To make fizz, substitute club soda for milk.

4

34491B-00

STRAWBERRY APPLE PUNCH

FSGA Women's Committee

2 qt. fresh Florida
  STRAWBERRIES
1 (2-L.) bottle ginger ale or
  Sprite

2 qt. apple juice
Mint leaves

Blend berries and 2 cups apple juice in a blender until smooth. Pour mixture into a punch bowl and add remaining juice, gingerale, and mix. Float on ice ring in bowl. Garnish glass with fresh whole berry.

STRAWBERRIES IN CHAMPAGNE

FSGA Women's Committee

1 qt. large Florida
  STRAWBERRIES
White dinner wine

Brandy
Champagne

Stem a quart of large strawberries. Do not wash; rinse with white dinner wine. Sprinkle with brandy; chill. Before serving, sprinkle with sugar. At the table, pour champagne over the berries; serve at once.

STRAWBERRY COLADA FLORIDIAN

FSGA Women's Committee

1 pt. Florida STRAWBERRIES
1/3 c. coconut cream

1/3 c. light rum
1 1/2 c. crushed ice

Reserve 4 strawberries for garnish, set aside. Hull and slice remaining strawberries. Place strawberries in electric blender and blend until smooth. Add coconut cream, rum and crushed ice. Blend until smooth. Pour into tall glasses. Garnish each glass with a reserved strawberry cut to resemble a fan. Makes 4 servings.

FRESH STRAWBERRY SODA

FSGA Women's Committee

1 pt. Florida STRAWBERRIES
1 T. instant dissolving sugar

3 c. club soda or seltzer, chilled

Hull and slice the strawberries. Place in electric blender with sugar. Blend until smooth. Pour 1/4 cup of the strawberry mixture into an 8-ounce glass for each serving. Fill glass with club soda, stir to mix. Makes 4 servings.

STRAWBERRY SUN BREAK

FSGA Women's Committee

1 pt. Florida STRAWBERRIES
1 c. milk
1 c. orange juice

½ banana
2 T. sugar
2 c. ice

Mix strawberries, milk, orange juice, banana, sugar and ice in an electric blender for approximately 30 seconds.

STRAWBERRY ICE CREAM SLUSH

FSGA Women's Committee

1 qt. fresh STRAWBERRIES,
  additional fresh
  STRAWBERRIES, opt.
2 c. nonfat vanilla ice cream,
  softened
1(3-oz.) pkg. sugar free
  strawberry gelatin

½ c. boiling water
2 tsp. lemon juice
2 L. diet lemon-lime soda,
  chilled

In a large bowl, mash strawberries, add ice cream. In a small bowl, dissolve gelatin in water; stir in lemon juice. Add to the strawberry mixture, mix well. Pour into a 1½-quart freezer container; cover and freeze overnight. Remove from freezer 15 minutes before serving. Spoon into glasses; add soda. Garnish with strawberries if desired. Yield: 10 servings.

STRAWBERRY PINEAPPLE SHAKE

FSGA Women's Committee

1 pt. Florida STRAWBERRIES   1 c. milk
1 can (20-oz.) pineapple chunks

Reserve 4 strawberries and 4 pineapple chunks for garnish. Hull remaining and slice. Drain pineapple. Place half of the strawberries and pineapple chunks in electric blender. Add ½ cup milk. Blend until smooth. Pour into 2 tall glasses. Repeat. Place a strawberry and pineapple chunk on 4 bamboo skewers. Makes 4 servings.

LOW CALORIE STRAWBERRY MILKSHAKE

FSGA Women's Committee

1-2 c. frozen unsweetened
  Florida STRAWBERRIES
2 c. low-fat milk

1 tsp. artificial sweetener
1 tsp. vanilla flavoring

Blend milk, sweetener and vanilla flavoring for 2 seconds. Add frozen strawberries, one at a time until the desired thickness. Makes 4 servings.

34491B-00

STRAWBERRY 7-UP SLUSH

FSGA Women's Committee

2 c. whole fresh
  STRAWBERRIES
1½ c. crushed ice

1 can 7-Up
2 T. sugar
½ c. water

Place in blender. Blend on high until slushy.

STRAWBERRY APPLE COOLER

FSGA Women's Committee

1⅔ c. Florida STRAWBERRY
  purée

4 c. apple juice
Crushed ice

Mix 2 cups of apple juice with the strawberry purée and mix in the blender until frothy. Add the rest of the apple juice, stir and pour into glasses about half filled with crushed ice. Yield: 6 servings.

STRAWBERRY EGG NOG

FSGA Women's Committee

1 c. fresh Florida
  STRAWBERRIES
3 c. heavy cream
1 qt. vanilla ice cream

8 egg yolks
¼ c. B & B liqueur
¼ c. Bacardi rum
Ground nutmeg

Combine all ingredients in a blender. Blend until thick and creamy. Sprinkle nutmeg on top when serving.

STRAWBERRY CLOUD

Reggie Gordon

1 c. fresh STRAWBERRIES,
  sliced
1 med. banana, cut up

½ c. milk
1 (8-oz.) ctn. strawberry low fat
  yogurt

In blender container, combine strawberries, banana, milk and yogurt. Cover and blend at medium speed 30-60 seconds or until smooth. Serve immediately.

FESTIVE STRAWBERRY CITRUS PUNCH

Reggie Gordon

1 pt. fresh Florida
  STRAWBERRIES, sliced
1 c. Florida sugar
3 c. boiling water
1¼ c. Florida orange juice

¼ c. Florida lime juice
2 c. unsweetened pineapple
  juice
1 (32-oz.) bottle ginger ale
Mint leaves, opt.

(continued)

Dissolve sugar in boiling water, stir in orange juice, lime juice, pineapple juice, and strawberries. Pour mixture into a plastic container. Place container in freezer until mixture becomes firm. Remove from freezer 1 hour before serving. Cut into small cubes and place into punch bowl. Add ginger ale; stir until slushy. Garnish with mint leaves if desired. Yield: approximately 20 servings. Champagne may be substituted for ginger ale.

STRAWBERRY PUNCH

Gayle Gilford

1 qt. fresh or frozen
  STRAWBERRIES
3 c. water
2 c. sugar
46-oz. can pineapple juice

1½ c. orange juice
¼ c. lemon juice
3 ripe bananas
3 qt. chilled ginger ale

Mix sugar and water in saucepan; bring to boil. Peel and break up bananas and put in blender jar with a little of the pineapple juice. Process until smooth. Combine and mix well sugar water, banana mixture, pineapple juice, crushed strawberries, orange and lemon juice. Pour into gallon jugs, cap and freeze. Leave 2 inches air space for expansion. When ready to use, let thaw (about 2½ hours) until slushy. Pour into punch bowl and add ginger ale and serve. Can add ½ gallon vanilla ice cream. Yield: 5 servings.

STRAWBERRY BANANA SMOOTHIE

FSGA Women's Committee

¾ lb. Florida STRAWBERRIES
2 c. ice cubes
1 sm. ripe banana

½ c. low fat vanilla yogurt
½ c. water
2 T. strawberry syrup

In blender purée all ingredients.

Recipe Favorites

34491B-00

All Dressed in Green

Sunny Florida Salad, page 9

Soups and Salads

ALL DRESSED IN GREEN

STRAWBERRY PRETZEL SALAD

Leota Mauersberg
Denise Enochs

3 c. sliced STRAWBERRIES
1½ sticks butter, softened
3 T. brown sugar
2½ c. crushed pretzels
1 (8-oz.) pkg. cream cheese

1 c. white sugar
8-oz. Cool Whip
1 lg. pkg. strawberry Jello
2 c. boiling water
½ c. cold water

Cream butter and brown sugar together. Add crushed pretzels. Press into a 9 x 13-inch buttered (lightly) pan. Bake at 350° for 10 minutes. Set aside to cool. Combine 1 (8-ounce) package cream cheese, softened, with 1 cup white sugar. Cream until smooth, fold in 8-ounces Cool Whip (6-ounces). Set aside. Dissolve 1 large package strawberry Jello in 2 cups boiling water. Then add ½ cup cold water. Stir in 3 cups sliced cold fresh strawberries into Jello mixture. Chill until partially congealed. Spread Jello mixture over cream cheese mixture. Return to refrigerator and chill until firm.

SUNNY FLORIDA SALAD

Erin Freel Best

1 pt. Florida STRAWBERRIES, stemmed and halved
4 fresh whole STRAWBERRIES
1 T. lemon juice
2 c. (10-12-oz.) cooked chicken, cut into 1-inch cubes
1 (20-oz.) can pineapple chunks, drained

1½ c. homemade or bottled sweet and spicy French dressing
1 lg. banana, sliced
½ c. chopped celery
Lettuce leaves
Crackers, sesame seeds, opt.

Sprinkle lemon juice over bananas in a large bowl. Add chicken, pineapple and strawberries. Toss to mix. Place lettuce leaves on individual serving plates. Top with salad mixture. Sprinkle with sesame seeds. Serve with dressing and crackers. Garnish with whole strawberries. Yield: 4 servings.

STRAWBERRY DESSERT SALAD

FSGA Women's Committee

2 c. chopped Florida STRAWBERRIES
8 oz. cream cheese, softened
¾ c. sugar
2 or 3 bananas, sliced

1 (20-oz.) can pineapple tidbits, drained
½ c. chopped walnuts
1 or 2 ctn. whipped topping

(continued)

Blend cream cheese and sugar in large bowl. Combine undrained straw-berries, bananas, pineapple, walnuts and whipped topping in bowl. Mix well. Add to cream cheese mixture; mix gently. Spoon into loaf pan. Freeze until firm. Slice and serve. Yield: 18 servings.

SUMMERTIME FROZEN FRUIT SALAD

Dave Gale

1½ c. sliced Florida
  STRAWBERRIES
8 oz. cream cheese, softened
¼ c. honey
2 med. bananas, sliced

1 c. miniature marshmallows
1 c. pineapple chunks
1 c. fresh cherries, pitted and
  halved
1 c. whipping cream, whipped

Beat cream cheese at medium speed of an electric mixer until smooth. Add honey, and beat well. Gently stir in strawberries, bananas, marsh-mallows, pineapple and cherries. Fold in whipped cream. Spoon mixture into a 9-inch square pan and freeze. Remove salad from freezer 30 minutes before serving. Yield: 9 servings.

FLORIDA FRUIT SALAD

FSGA Women's Committee

3 c. whole fresh Florida
  STRAWBERRIES
6 sm. heads Boston or Bibb
  lettuce

2 c. seedless white grapes
1 c. pecans, coarsely chopped

Dressing:

2 T. honey 2 T. lemon juice ¼ c. mayonnaise ½ c. whipping cream

Wash each head of lettuce, wrap them in a towel and refrigerate for at least 1 hour. Wash and hull Florida strawberries. Drain them on a towel. Cut each strawberry in half. Pull the systems from the grapes and wash and drain the grapes. Mix them in a larger bowl with the strawberries and pecans. Mix together the honey, lemon juice and mayonnaise and put over fruit mixture. Whip the cream until it holds soft round peaks. Fold into fruit salad. Pull each head of lettuce open to make a leafy bowl. Pile the salad into the lettuce, make in six individual servings, serve immediately.

34491B-00

FLORIDA STRAWBERRY-BANANA SALAD WITH SESAME

FSGA Women's Committee

3 c. whole fresh Florida
  STRAWBERRIES
3 med. bananas

1 tsp. lemon juice
Lettuce leaves
1/4 c. toasted sesame seeds

Dressing:

1/3 c. mayonnaise
2 T. sour cream

2 T. milk

Peel and slice bananas. Sprinkle them with lemon juice. Wash and hull the Florida strawberries and mix them with the bananas. Make the dressing by stirring together the mayonnaise, sour cream and milk. Pour over bananas and strawberries and mix carefully. Arrange the salad on a bed of lettuce leaves and mix liberally with sesame seeds. Plan to serve salad shortly after you mix it so the bananas wont get dark and mushy. Yields: 6 servings.

STRAWBERRY CONGEALED SALAD

Gayle Gilford

1 1/2 c. fresh STRAWBERRIES,
  cut in half
1 box strawberry Jello
1/2 pt. whipping cream

1/2 c. sharp cheese, grated
2/3 c. pecans, chopped fine
1/4 c. coconut
1 1/2 c. hot water

Mix Jello in 1 1/2 cup hot water. Refrigerate until it starts to jell. Whip cream and fold into Jello. Add cheese, pineapple, pecans, coconut and strawberries, mix well. Put in 8-inch square pan and refrigerate until set. Cut into squares to serve. Keeps in refrigerator for several days.

STRAWBERRY SALAD

Faye Wetherington

1 pt. Florida STRAWBERRIES,
  sliced lengthwise
3/4 c. fresh or canned water
  chestnuts, peeled thinly sliced
3 or 4 shallots, minced
1 qt. sm. spinach leaves,
  stemmed and torn
1 qt. garden lettuce, cut in
  narrow strips

3 T. hazelnut oil
1 T. raspberry vinegar
Salt and pepper, freshly ground
2 sm. navel oranges, peeled,
  sliced crosswise and cut in
  half

Blanch the water chestnuts for two minutes in boiling water and immediately refresh in cold water. Combine with greens and shallots. Add oil and toss. Add vinegar, salt and pepper. Add fruit and gently toss again.

STRAWBERRY SALAD

Linda Atkins

1 pkg. frozen STRAWBERRIES
2 (3-oz.) pkg. strawberry Jello
2½ c. boiling water

28 lg. marshmallows
1 med. can crushed pineapple

Mix Jello in hot water, add marshmallows, cut in small pieces. Stir until Jello is dissolved. Add pineapple and strawberries. Chill until firm. Serve with whipped cream.

Recipe Note: You can use miniature marshmallows. Also you can use 2 packages of strawberries in place of pineapple if you prefer.

BABY BLUE SALAD

FSGA Women's Committee

1 pt. fresh STRAWBERRIES,
 quartered
¾ lb. mixed salad greens
Balsamic vinaigrette

4 oz. blue cheese, crumbled
2 oranges, peeled and thinly
 sliced
Sweet & spicy pecans

Toss greens with Balsamic vinaigrette and blue cheese. Place on 6 individual plates. Arrange orange slices over greens; sprinkle with strawberries, and top with sweet and spicy pecans.

FLORIDA STRAWBERRY SALAD

Erin Freel Best

16 oz. frozen STRAWBERRIES
1 lg. pkg. strawberry Jello
2 c. hot water
1 sm. can crushed pineapple
 juice

2 bananas
8 oz. sour cream

Combine Jello and boiling water until dissolved. Add strawberries, pineapple and bananas. Divide in half. Congeal half and then cover with sour cream, pour other half of strawberry mix over cream. Congeal.

34491B-00

FIESTA TOSSED SALAD

Teresa Griffin

1 c. STRAWBERRIES
1 head romaine lettuce, washed
  and torn
1 c. celery, finely chopped
2-4 green onion tops, finely
  chopped

1 orange, peeled and sectioned,
  mandarin oranges may be
  substituted
½ c. chopped pecans

Fiesta Dressing:

½ tsp. Kosher salt
Dash of pepper
¼ c. olive oil

2 tsp. sugar
2 tsp. white wine vinegar
Dash of Tabasco

Combine lettuce, celery and onion in large bowl, toss and chill. Just before serving toss in remaining ingredients. **Dressing:**Combine all ingredients in Mason jar, shake well. Chill 2-3 hours before using. Makes about ½ cup.

STRAWBERRY CONGEALED SALAD

FSGA Women's Committee

1½ c. fresh Florida
  STRAWBERRIES, cut in half
1 box strawberry gelatin
½ pt. whipping cream

½ c. sharp cheddar cheese
½ c. crushed pineapple, drained
⅔ c. pecans, cut fine
¼ c. coconut

Mix gelatin in 1½ cups hot water. Put in refrigerator until it starts to thicken. Whip cream and fold into gelatin, add cheddar cheese, pineapple, pecans, coconut and strawberries. Mix well. Refrigerate in 8-inch square baking dish until set. Cut into squares. Serve on a bed of lettuce. Garnish with fresh whole Florida strawberries. Keep refrigerated.

FLORIDA STRAWBERRY FRUIT MOLD

FSGA Women's Committee

2 c. Florida sliced
  STRAWBERRIES
1 env. unflavored gelatin
¼ c. cold water
1½ c. pineapple juice
½ c. orange juice
2 tsp. mixed pickling spices
1 T. sugar

1 T. lemon juice
1 c. pineapple chunks, drained
¼ c. white grapes
Fresh mint leaves, grapes and
  Florida STRAWBERRIES for
  garnish
Lettuce

Soften the gelatin in the cold water. In a saucepan combine the pineapple and orange juices, pickling spices, and sugar. Bring just to a boil and simmer 2 minutes. Remove the spices. Add the softened gelatin

(continued)

to the hot juice stirring until dissolved. Add the lemon juice. Chill until the gelatin is about half set. Then fold in the pineapple, Florida strawberries and grapes. Pour into an oiled 4-cup mold. Chill at least 3 hours. To serve, unmold onto a serving plate covered with lettuce leaves and garnish with fresh mint leaves, a few grapes and whole strawberries. Makes 6-8 servings.

FLORIDA STRAWBERRY SOUP

FSGA Women's Committee

2 c. sliced Florida
 STRAWBERRIES
1 c. milk
2 T. instant nonfat dry milk
1 c. light cream

2 T. honey
1 tsp. cinnamon
Whole Florida STRAWBERRIES
 for garnish

Purée the strawberries in a blender or food processor. Gradually add the milk, dry milk, cream, honey and cinnamon, processing continuously. Chill before serving. Garnish each serving with several whole Florida strawberries. Yield: 6 servings.

CHILLED STRAWBERRY SOUP

Erin Freel Best

2 c. fresh STRAWBERRIES
1 c. water, divided
1 c. apple juice
²/₃ c. sugar
¹/₂ tsp. ground cinnamon
¹/₈ tsp. ground cloves

2 (8-oz.) ctn. low fat strawberry
 yogurt
2-3 drops red food color
Low fat dairy sour cream for
 garnish

In medium saucepan, combine ³/₄ cup water, apple juice, sugar, cinnamon and cloves. Cook over medium heat until mixture boils. Cool. In blender, combine strawberries and remaining ¹/₄ cup of water; blend until smooth. In large mixing bowl, combine apple juice mixture, puréed strawberries and yogurt. Whisk to combine evenly. Cover; refrigerate until well chilled. To serve pour into chilled individual serving dishes; garnish with sour cream.

STRAWBERRY & SPINACH SALAD

Reggie Gordon

1 c. fresh STRAWBERRIES,
 sliced
4 c. fresh spinach leaves, torn,
 washed and dried

¹/₄ c. light sour cream
2 T. honey
1 tsp. lime juice
Dash of nutmeg

(continued)

14

Florida Strawberry Festival
2008

GENERAL ADMISSION ADULT
$10.00

03/05/08 FSF:046
Tck 333 Trn 74

Powered by OmniTicket Network
www.OmniTicket.com

ADULT

Florida Strawberry Festival

GENERAL ADMISSION ADULT

ADULT

Gently toss spinach and strawberries in salad bowl. In small bowl, combine sour cream, honey, lime juice and nutmeg; blend well. Pour dressing over salad and toss gently.

STRAWBERRY RHUBARB SALAD

FSGA Women's Committee

2 c. sliced fresh
  STRAWBERRIES
4 c. diced rhubarb
1½ c. water
½ c. sugar

1 pkg. strawberry gelatin
1 c. orange juice
1 T. grated orange peel
Lettuce leaves, opt.
Strawberries for garnish, opt.

Combine rhubarb, water and sugar in a saucepan, cook until tender. Place gelatin in a glass bowl; add hot rhubarb mixture and stir until gelatin dissolves completely. Add orange juice and peel. Chill until syrupy; fold in strawberries. Pour into an oiled 1-quart mold; chill until set. Unmold onto lettuce leaves and garnish with strawberries if desired.

STRAWBERRY-GLAZED FRUIT SALAD

FSGA Women's Committee

1 qt. fresh STRAWBERRIES,
  halved
1 can unsweetened pineapple
  chunks, drained

4 firm bananas, sliced
1 jar or pouch strawberry glaze

In a large bowl, gently toss strawberries, pineapple, and bananas; fold in the glaze. Chill for 1 hour.

STRAWBERRY CINDY

FSGA Women's Committee

1 pt. fresh sliced
  STRAWBERRIES
2 (3-oz.) pkgs. strawberry
  gelatin

2½ c. boiling water
3 bananas, sliced
½ c. chopped pecans
1 c. sour cream

Dissolve gelatin in boiling water in bowl. Stir in strawberries. Add bananas and pecans, mix gently. Spoon half the mixture into 8 x 8-inch dish. Chill until firm. Chill remaining gelatin mixture until partially set. Layer sour cream and partially congealed gelatin over congealed layer. Chill until firm. Yield: 9 servings.

STRAWBERRY EASTER SALAD

FSGA Women's Committee

2 pt. fresh sliced
  STRAWBERRIES
1 (6-oz.) pkg. strawberry gelatin
2 c. boiling water
1 (8-oz.) can crushed pineapple,
  drained

2 bananas, chopped
8-oz. cream cheese, softened
1 c. confectioners' sugar
1 tsp. vanilla extract
1 c. whipping cream, whipped
½ c. finely chopped pecans

Dissolve gelatin in boiling water in bowl. Remove and reserve ¼ cup gelatin mixture. Add strawberries, pineapple and bananas to remaining gelatin; mix well. Spoon into 9 x 13-inch dish. Chill until firm. Combine cream cheese and confectioners' sugar in mixer bowl; beat until smooth. Add vanilla and whipped cream; mix gently. Stir in reserved gelatin. Spread over congealed layer; sprinkle with pecans. Chill overnight. Yield: 15 servings.

STRAWBERRY SALAD

FSGA Women's Committee

1 pt. fresh sliced
  STRAWBERRIES
2 (3-oz.) pkgs. strawberry
  gelatin

2 c. boiling water
1 (8-oz.) can crushed pineapple
½ c. pecans
1 c. sour cream

Dissolve gelatin in boiling water in bowl. Add strawberries, undrained pineapple and pecans; mix well. Spoon half the mixture into salad mold. Chill until firm. Spread sour cream over congealed layer. Spread remaining gelatin evenly over sour cream. Chill until firm. Unmold onto serving plate. Yield: 10 servings.

THREE-LAYER STRAWBERRY SALAD

FSGA Women's Committee

2½ c. STRAWBERRIES
1½ c. flour
¾ c. melted butter
½ c. pecans
8 oz. cream cheese, softened
1 c. confectioners' sugar

8 oz. whipped topping
2 (3-oz.) pkgs. strawberry
  gelatin
2 c. boiling water
Ice cubes
1 c. pecans

Combine flour, melted butter and ½ cup pecans in bowl; mix well. Spread in 9 x 13-inch dish. Bake at 375° until light brown. Cool to room temperature. Combine cream cheese and confectioners' sugar in mixer bowl; beat until smooth. Mix in 1 cup of whipped topping. Spread over baked layer. Dissolve gelatin in boiling water in bowl. Stir in ice cubes using package directions for fast setting. Stir in strawberries. Spoon

(continued)

34491B-00

over cream cheese layer. Chill until firm. Top with remaining whipped topping; sprinkle with ½ cup pecans. Chill till serving time.

STRAWBERRY SOUP

FSGA Women's Committee

2 c. STRAWBERRIES, sliced
1 c. sour cream
1 c. half & half
¼ c. sugar

2 T. brandy
½ tsp. vanilla extract
STRAWBERRY fans or slices

Combine sliced strawberries, sour cream, half & half, sugar, brandy and vanilla in container of an electric blender. Process until smooth. Pour into chilled soup bowls; garnish each serving with a strawberry fan or strawberry slices. Yield: 3½ cups.

ROSE WINE STRAWBERRY SOUP

FSGA Women's Committee

2 c. sliced fresh
  STRAWBERRIES
1 c. sour cream
1 c. medium cream

⅓ c. sugar
½ c. orange juice
½ c. rose wine

Blend all ingredients in a food processor or blender until smooth. Serve chilled as a soup or a dessert. Garnish with fresh mint.

Recipe Favorites

Recipe Favorites

34491B-00

Shortcakes, Breads and Spreads

Florida Strawberry Shortcake

Strawberry breads, muffins, shortcakes, butters, jams, jellies, preserves and marmalades

SHORTCAKES, BREADS & SPREADS

TOUCH OF SPRING MUFFINS

Megan Freel

½ c. sliced fresh
STRAWBERRIES
2 c. all-purpose flour
½ c. sugar
1 T. baking powder

½ tsp. salt
1 egg
¾ c. milk
⅓ c. vegetable oil
½ c. sliced fresh rhubarb

Topping:

6 sm. fresh STRAWBERRIES,
halved

2 tsp. sugar

In a large bowl, combine flour, sugar, baking powder and salt. In another bowl, beat egg, milk and oil until smooth. Stir into the dry ingredients just until moistened. Fold in strawberries and rhubarb. Fill greased or paper lined muffin cups ¾ full. Place a strawberry half, cut side down on each. Sprinkle with sugar. Bake at 375° for 22-25 minutes before removing from pan to a wire rack. Serve warm. Yield: 1 dozen.

WALK OF FAME CHOCOLATE STAR SHORTCAKES

FSGA Women's Committee

2 (1-pt.) baskets
STRAWBERRIES, hulled,
halved, lightly sugared
2 c. all-purpose flour
½ c. sugar
⅓ c. unsweetened cocoa
powder
1 tsp. baking powder
½ tsp. baking soda
½ tsp. salt

1 c. (6 oz.) semi-sweet chocolate
chips
1⅔ to 1¾ c. chilled whipping
cream
Melted, unsalted butter
Additional sugar
Purchased chocolate sauce
1 c. chilled whipping cream,
whipped
Fresh mint sprigs, opt.

Preheat oven to 325°. Sift flour, ½ cup sugar, cocoa, baking powder, baking soda, and salt into large bowl. Mix in chocolate chips. Mix in just enough chilled cream to form dough that will be firm enough to roll out. Turn out dough onto well floured work surface. Using well floured hands, pat dough to ¾-inch thick rectangle, frequently sliding long knife under dough to prevent sticking. With floured 2-inch star shaped cookie cutter, cut out stars. Gather dough scraps; pat out to ¾-inch thick rectangle and cut out additional stars for total of about 24. Brush stars with butter, sprinkle with additional sugar. Arrange shortcake stars sugared side down on 2 heavy large baking sheets. Brush tops with butter and sprinkle with sugar. Bake until shortcakes feel firm and tester inserted into center comes out with few moist crumbs, about 22 minutes. Transfer shortcakes to rack and cool. Place scoop of ice cream in each

(continued)

of 8 bowls. Garnish with sauce, berries, whipped cream and 1 or 2 stars and mint, if desired. Serve immediately. Serves 8.

STRAWBERRY CREAM CHEESE SPREAD

1 c. STRAWBERRIES, chopped
1 (8-oz.) pkg. cream cheese,
  softened

1/4 c. pecans, chopped fine
1/2 c. powdered sugar
1 tsp. lemon juice

Combine cream cheese and powdered sugar and beat until light and fluffy. Add strawberries, pecans and lemon juice, blending well. Chill several hours. Delicious on crackers or bread.

STRAWBERRY ICING

FSGA Women's Committee

2 c. STRAWBERRIES, chopped
1 egg white

1 c. sugar

Save one cup sliced berries for garnish. Combine all ingredients in mixing bowl. Beat on high speed until stiff. Icing will cover a large cake. Garnish with sliced or whole berries.

STRAWBERRY CREAM CHEESE SPREAD

FSGA Women's Committee

1 c. sliced fresh Florida
STRAWBERRIES or 2/3 c.
unsweetened STRAWBERRY
purée

1 (8-oz.) pkg. cream cheese

Beat together the cream cheese and Florida strawberries until the mixture is creamy. (A food processor is the easiest way.) Chill overnight to develop flavor. Use for sandwich filling.

Variation: Strawberry Nut Spread. Add 2 tablespoons milk and 1/2 cup finely chopped nuts to make a strawberry nut spread.

LO-CAL STRAWBERRY REFRIGERATOR JAM

FSGA Women's Committee

2 c. fresh sliced
  STRAWBERRIES
6 T. sugar or sugar substitute
2 T. lemon juice

3 T. cold water
1 T. plain gelatin
1 1/2 tsp. cornstarch

Combine lemon juice, water, gelatin, and cornstarch in saucepan. Wait one minute, then heat gently until gelatin dissolves, stirring constantly.

(continued)

Add strawberries and sugar (if used) and heat to boil. Simmer, stirring constantly for 3 minutes. Remove from heat and add sugar substitute (if used). Stir until dissolved. Refrigerate in covered jars. Must be kept in refrigerator.

FOUR-BERRY SPREAD

FSGA Women's Committee

1½ c. fresh STRAWBERRIES
1½ c. fresh raspberries
1 c. fresh blackberries

1 c. fresh blueberries
1 pkg. powdered fruit pectin
7 c. sugar

Crush berries in a large kettle, mix in sugar. Stir in pectin; bring to a rolling boil. Boil for 1 minute, stirring constantly. Remove from the heat; skim off any foam. Ladle hot mixture into hot jars, leaving ¼-inch head space. Adjust caps. Process for 10 minutes in a boiling water bath.

FREEZER STRAWBERRY JAM

EvaNell Griffin

3 c. fresh STRAWBERRIES
5 c. sugar
1 (1¾-oz.) pkg. powdered fruit
  pectin

1 c. water

Remove stems for strawberries; rinse and drain. Purée strawberries in container of electric blender; combine purée and sugar, stirring well. Set aside 10 minutes. Stir pectin into water. Bring to a boil; boil 1 minute. Pour pectin mixture into purée; stir 3 minutes. Ladle into sterilized freezer jars, sealing at once with metal lids, or ladle into frozen food containers and seal at once with plastic lids. Allow to stand at room temperature for 24 hours. Store in freezer. Yield: about 3 pints.

DANA'S QUICK & EASY STRAWBERRY JAM

Dana Telese

1 qt. ripe STRAWBERRIES,
  mashed
4 c. sugar

¾ c. water
1 box Sure-Jell fruit pectin

Measure 2 cups mashed strawberries into bowl. (Save any remaining fruit for another use.) Stir in sugar. Let stand 10 minutes, stirring occasionally. Mix water and pectin in small saucepan. Bring to boil on high heat, stirring constantly. Continue boiling and stirring for 1 minute. Stir into fruit mixture. Stir 3 minutes or until sugar is completely dissolved. Fill plastic containers quickly to within ½ inch of tops, cover with lids. Let stand at room temperature for 24 hours. Jam is ready to use. Refrigerate up to 3 weeks or freeze up to 1 year. Thaw in refrigerator.

STRAWBERRY MARMALADE

FSGA Women's Committee

1 qt. fresh STRAWBERRIES, crushed	½ c. water
2 med. oranges	⅛ tsp. baking soda
2 med. lemons	7 c. sugar
	1 pouch liquid fruit pectin

Peel outer layer of oranges and lemons. Set aside. Cut between the membrane to remove each section. Set the fruit and juice aside; discard membrane, chop peels; place in a large saucepan. Add water and baking soda; cover and bring to a boil. Reduce heat; simmer for 10 minutes. Add sectioned fruit and juice to saucepan; cover and simmer for 20 minutes. Add strawberries. Measure fruit; return 4 cups to the saucepan. (If more than 4 cups, discard any extra; if less add water to equal 4 cups.) Add sugar and mix well. Boil uncovered for 5 minutes. Add pectin, stirring until mixture boils. Boil for 1 minute. Remove from the heat; skim off foam. Pour hot mixture into hot half-pint jars or freezer containers, leaving ¼-inch headspace. Adjust caps. Process for 10 minutes in a boiling water bath or store in the freezer.

BANANA & STRAWBERRY JAM

Dee Dee Grooms

4 c. prepared fruit, about 1½ qt. full ripe STRAWBERRIES & 3 ripe bananas	2 T. lemon juice, 1 lemon
	5 c. (2¼ lb.) sugar
	1 box Sure-Jell fruit pectin

First prepare the fruit. Crush completely, one layer at a time, about 1½ quarts strawberries. Mash 3 bananas to a fine pulp. Combine fruits and measure 4 cups into a large saucepan. Add lemon juice. Then make the jam. Measure sugar and set aside. Mix fruit pectin into fruit in saucepan. Place over high heat and stir until mixture comes to a hard boil. Immediately add all sugar and stir. Bring to a full rolling boil and boil hard 1 minute, stirring constantly. Remove from heat and skim off foam with metal spoon. Then stir and skim for 5 minutes to cool slightly and prevent floating fruit. Ladle quickly into glasses. Cover at once with ⅛ inch hot paraffin.

STRAWBERRY PINEAPPLE JAM

Dee Dee Grooms

1 (10-oz.) pkg. Birds Eye quick thaw STRAWBERRIES, thawed	¼ c. water
	3½ c. (1½ lb.) sugar
1 can (20-oz.) crushed pineapple	1 box Sure-Jell fruit pectin

First prepare the fruit. Thoroughly crush the berries. Measure 1 cup strawberries and juice into a large saucepan; add pineapple and water. Then make the jam. Measure sugar and set aside. Mix fruit pectin into

(continued)

34491B-00

fruit saucepan. Place over high heat and stir until mixture comes to a hard boil. Immediately add all sugar and stir. Bring to a full rolling boil and boil hard 1 minute, stirring constantly. Remove from heat and skim off foam with a metal spoon. Then stir and skim for 5 minutes to cool slightly and prevent floating fruit. Ladle quickly into glasses. Cover at once with 1/8 inch hot paraffin. Makes about 5½ cups or 7 glasses.

RASPBERRY & STRAWBERRY JELLY

Dee Dee Grooms

4 c. prepared juice, about 1½ qt. each fully ripe red raspberries and

STRAWBERRIES
7½ c. (3¼ lb.) sugar
2 pouches Certo fruit pectin

First prepare the juice. Crush thoroughly or grind about 1½ quarts each full ripe raspberries and strawberries. Place in jelly cloth or bag and squeeze out juice. Measure 4 cups juice into a very large saucepan. Then make the jelly. Add sugar to juice; mix well. Place over high heat; bring to a boil, stirring constantly. Remove from heat, skim off foam with a metal spoon, and pour quickly into glasses. Cover at once with 1/8 inch hot paraffin. Makes about 7¼ cups.

STRAWBERRY SAUTERNE PRESERVES

Dee Dee Grooms

4 c. prepared fruit, about 1 qt. fully ripe STRAWBERRIES
4½ c. (2 lbs.) sugar

1/4 c. sauterne wine
1 box Sure-Jell fruit pectin
1/2 c. water

First, prepare the fruit. Measure 4 cups (firmly packed without crushing) firm ripe small strawberries. (If berries are large, halve them.) Layer berries and sugar in a large saucepan. Add wine. Let stand at room temperature 4-5 hours. Then make the preserves. Place the fruit mixture over medium heat, bring to a full rolling boil, and boil hard 2 minutes, stirring constantly. Mix into hot fruit. Skim off foam with metal spoon. Ladle quickly into jars, leaving 1/8 inch space at top. Process in water bath.

CURRANT & STRAWBERRY JAM

Dee Dee Grooms

4½ c. juice, about 1½ qt. each fully ripe red currants & STRAWBERRIES

1/2 c. water
6 c. (2 lbs. 10-oz.) sugar
1 box Sure-Jell fruit pectin

First, prepare the juice. Stem and crush thoroughly about 1½ quarts full ripe red currants. Add the water; bring to a boil and simmer, covered 10 minutes. Crush thoroughly about 1½ quarts fully ripe strawberries.

(continued)

Place fruits in jelly cloth or bag; squeeze out juice. Measure 4½ cups into a very large saucepan. Then make the jelly. Measure sugar and set aside. Add Sure-Jell fruit pectin to juice and mix well. Place over high heat and stir until mixture comes to a hard boil. At once stir in sugar. Bring to a full rolling boil and boil hard 1 minute, stirring constantly. Remove from heat, skim off foam with a metal spoon, and pour quickly into glasses. Cover at once with ⅛ inch paraffin. Makes about 6½ cups.

STRAWBERRY PINEAPPLE MARMALADE

EvaNell Griffin

1½ qt. STRAWBERRIES
2½ c. finely chopped (about 1
  med.) fresh pineapple
1 tsp. grated orange rind

2½ c. chopped orange pulp,
  about 4 med. oranges
7 c. sugar

Combine pineapple, orange rind and pulp, and sugar in a large saucepan. Cook over medium heat, stirring occasionally, until mixture boils and sugar dissolves; boil 15 minutes. Add strawberries and boil until thick, about 20-30 minutes, stirring frequently. Pour quickly into sterilized jars. Cover at once with metal lids and screw bands tight. Process jars in boiling water bath for 10 minutes. Yield: 3 pints.

STRAWBERRY ITALIAN CREAM

Susan Kurchinski

2 pt. Florida STRAWBERRIES,
  puréed
1 doz. champagne biscuits
4 T. chocolate liqueur
4 T. Amaretto liqueur
4 T. whipping cream

2 oz. cream cheese
4 T. powdered sugar
9 oz. whipped topping
Fresh whole Florida
  STRAWBERRIES, garnish

Combine chocolate and Amaretto liqueur. Drizzle liqueurs over champagne biscuits; allow to soak in completely. In a a 1½-quart dish layer 4 champagne biscuits. In a separate bowl combine cream cheese, whipping cream and powdered sugar. Blend until mixed well. Spread a layer over biscuits. Top with a layer of puréed Florida strawberries. Repeat layers ending with berries. Top with whipped topping and fresh Florida strawberries. Best if chilled at least 1 hour.

SIMPLY IRRESISTIBLE STRAWBERRY SHORTBREAD

FSGA Women's Committee

Strawberry Sauce:

2 qt. Florida STRAWBERRIES, divided, 1st qt. stemmed, cleaned, mashed; 2nd qt. stemmed, cleaned, sliced

1 c. sugar
2 T. strawberry preserves
1 T. water

Shortbread:

2/3 c. confectioners' sugar
2 c. unbleached all-purpose flour

1/2 lb. (2 sticks) sweet butter, chilled
1 T. fresh lemon zest

Filling:

6-oz. pkg. cream cheese, softened
1/4 c. confectioners' sugar

1 T. half & half cream
1 tsp. lemon juice

Maple Nuts:

1 c. walnuts, toasted in 350° oven 7 minutes, then coarsely chopped

1/3 c. maple or maple flavored syrup

Strawberry Sauce: Combine first quart of mashed berries with sugar in saucepan. Bring to a boil over medium high heat then reduce heat to medium low and simmer 10 minutes stirring frequently. Skim foam. Remove from heat. Stir in preserves. In small cup mix cornstarch and water; add to berry sauce. Return pan to stove and cook until thickened, stirring constantly. Remove from heat and reserve. There should be about 2 cups of strawberry sauce. **Short Bread:**Preheat oven to 350°. Sift confectioners' sugar and flour together into food processor bowl fitted with steel blade. Cut each stick of butter into 8 pats. Sprinkle pats onto dry ingredients. Pulse on and off until fine crumbs form, about 30 pulses. Or if food processor is not available, use pastry blender or 2 knives to cut butter into flour. Stir in lemon zest. Pat crumbs into bottom of lightly greased 9 x 13-inch pan.

(continued)

Note: Mixture will be very dry. Bake on middle rack of oven for 30 minutes. Open oven door and spread 1 cup of strawberry sauce onto shortbread. Close oven door and continue to bake for 15 minutes. Remove shortbread from oven and cool. **Filling:** Beat cream cheese, confectioners' sugar, half & half and lemon juice together with electric mixer on high until well blended and creamy. Set aside. **Maple Nuts:** Combine walnuts and syrup. To assemble mix remaining quart of sliced strawberries with the remaining cup of strawberry sauce; spoon onto cooled shortbread. Dollop spread or pipe cream cheese topping on strawberry layer. Sprinkle with maple walnuts. May be served immediately or chilled. Keeps well for a couple of days. (Best if chilled 30 minutes to 1 hour.)

Note: Walnuts and strawberry sauce may be made 1 day in advance. Yields 12 generous servings.

OLD FASHION SHORTCAKE BISCUITS

Erin Freel Best

1½ qt. STRAWBERRIES
2½ c. sifted flour
2 tsp. baking powder
¼ tsp. soda
¾ tsp. salt
4 heaping T. Crisco shortening

Enough buttermilk to make
  dough
1 T. honey
1 egg white
Sugar to taste

Mix together dry ingredients, cut in shortening and add buttermilk. Mix well. Roll out thick on dough board. Will make 2 large or 4 medium biscuits. Beat honey and egg whites together, brush on biscuits. Bake at 450° until done. Prepare strawberries, slice or chop, add sugar to taste and let stand at least 30 minutes. Spoon over biscuits and top with Cool Whip or whipped cream.

STRAWBERRY ORANGE STREUSEL BREAD

FSGA Women's Committee

1½ c. chopped Florida
  STRAWBERRIES
1½ c. plus 2 T. cake flour, sifted
¾ tsp. baking powder
½ tsp. salt
1 c. granulated sugar

½ c. pecans, chopped
1½ tsp. orange zest, packed
  firmly
2 lg. eggs
½ c. Wesson oil
¼ c. orange juice

Preheat oven to 350°. Grease and flour a loaf pan. In a large bowl, mix flour, baking powder, salt, sugar, pecans, orange zest and strawberries; mix until blended. In small bowl mix eggs, oil and orange juice: add it to the flour mixture. Stir just until the dry ingredients are moist.

(continued)

34491B-00

Streusel Topping:

¼ c. all-purpose flour
¼ tsp. cinnamon

2 T. sugar
2 T. butter, room temperature

In another small bowl, combine flour, sugar and cinnamon. Cut butter in with a pastry cutter or fork. Set mixture aside. Pour batter into loaf pan and sprinkle with streusel topping. Bake 350° for 60-75 minutes or until tooth pick comes out clean. After 30 minutes of baking, tent with foil to prevent over browning. Remove from oven and place onto a cooling rack. Run a knife around the edge to loosen bread. Let cool 15 minutes before removing bread from the pan. Cool thoroughly before cutting. Store unused portions in the refrigerator. Garnish with whipped cream and sliced strawberries. Yield: 12-14 (½-inch) slices.

BANANA STRAWBERRY BREAD

Dee Dee Grooms

½ c. mashed fresh
  STRAWBERRIES, 7-8 berries
¾ c. sugar
½ c. margarine, softened or
  butter
2 eggs
½ c. mashed bananas, 1 banana

⅓ c. milk
1 tsp. vanilla
2 c. all-purpose flour
1 tsp. baking soda
½ tsp. salt
½ c. chopped nuts, if desired

Heat oven to 350°. Grease bottom only of 9 x 5-inch or 8 x 4-inch loaf pan. In large bowl beat sugar and margarine until light and fluffy. Beat in eggs. Add bananas, strawberries, milk, and vanilla; blend well. In small bowl, combine flour, nuts, baking soda and salt; mix well. Add to banana mixture; stir just until dry ingredients are moistened. Pour into greased pan. Bake at 350° for 50-60 minutes or until toothpick comes out clean. Cool completely and refrigerate.

FLORIDA STRAWBERRY SWEET BREAD

FSGA Women's Committee

2 c. Florida STRAWBERRIES
3 c. flour
1 tsp. salt
1½ tsp. cinnamon
2 c. sugar

1 tsp. soda
1 (3-oz.) pkg. strawberry gelatin
4 eggs, beaten
1¼ c. oil
1¼ c. nuts

Mix together flour, salt, cinnamon, sugar, gelatin, soda, reserving ¼ cup. Beat eggs and oil together. Fold in dry ingredients; add strawberries, mix the reserved ¼ cup dry ingredients with nuts. Fold into mixture. Pour into 2 greased loaf pans. Bake at 350° for 1 hour.

STRAWBERRY YOGURT MINI MUFFINS

Margaret Rodwell

1 c. chopped fresh STRAWBERRIES	½ tsp. salt
2 c. flour	2 eggs
½ c. sugar	1 c. plain yogurt
1½ tsp. baking soda	4 T. butter or margarine, melted
	1 tsp. vanilla

Heat oven at 350°. Grease 12-cup muffin tin. Combine dry ingredients. In another bowl beat eggs, yogurt, butter and vanilla until blended. Toss strawberries with dry ingredients. Stir egg mix into dry ingredients until flour is moistened. Spoon into tins. Bake 20-30 minutes.

STRAWBERRY PECAN STREUSEL MUFFINS

Rose Peacock

1¼ c. STRAWBERRIES, diced	1 egg
1½ c. unbleached flour	½ c. butter
½ c. maple sugar	½ c. water
¼ tsp. salt	1 tsp. lemon zest
1 tsp. cinnamon	

Topping:

½ c. pecans, chopped	1 tsp. cinnamon
½ c. maple sugar	1 tsp. lemon zest
¼ c. unbleached flour	2 tsp. margarine

Creaming method and fill sprayed muffin pan ⅔. Sprinkle topping on top of each muffin and bake at 375° for approximately 20 minutes.

FLORIDA STRAWBERRY CREAM CHEESE MUFFINS

FSGA Women's Committee

1 c. chopped Florida STRAWBERRIES	3 eggs
1 T. sugar	½ c. vegetable oil
2 c. all-purpose flour	½ c. milk
¾ c. sugar	1 tsp. grated orange rind
2 tsp. baking powder	8 oz. cream cheese
1 tsp. salt	¼ c. crushed Florida STRAWBERRIES

Sprinkle chopped strawberries with 1 tablespoon sugar, set aside. Sift together flour, sugar, baking powder and salt. Beat eggs in small bowl until light. Blend in oil, milk and orange rind. Add flour to mixture; stir for 10-15 strokes until mixed. Drain chopped berries; fold into batter. Fill paper lined muffin cups ⅔ full. Bake at 400° for 15 minutes. Serve warm with cream cheese mixed with crushed strawberries. Yield: 1 dozen.

34491B-00

STRAWBERRY ALMOND BISCUITS

Rose Peacock

1 c. fresh or frozen
  STRAWBERRIES, thawed and
  well drained
3 c. all-purpose flour
1 T. baking powder
½ tsp. baking soda
⅛ tsp. salt

½ c. sugar
¾ c. butter, cut in pieces
½ c. chopped almonds
¾ c. milk
¾ c. plain yogurt
1½ tsp. grated orange rind

Combine flour, baking powder, baking soda, salt, and sugar, cut in butter with pastry blender until mixture is crumbly. Stir in strawberries, almonds and orange rind. Add milk and yogurt, stirring with a fork until dry ingredients are moistened. (Dough will be very sticky.) Turn dough out onto a heavily floured surface, and knead lightly 5 or 6 times. Roll to ¾-inch thickness; cut with a 2½-inch round cutter. Place on a lightly greased baking sheet. Bake at 400° for 20-25 minutes or until lightly browned. Yield: 20 biscuits.

STRAWBERRY BREAD

Faye Wetherington

3 c. sliced Florida
  STRAWBERRIES
3 c. flour
1 tsp. strawberry flavoring
2 c. sugar
1 tsp. salt

1 c. chopped pecans
1 tsp. soda
½ tsp. cinnamon
1¼ c. oil
4 eggs
1 tsp. vanilla flavoring

In a large bowl, mix all dry ingredients together. In a medium bowl, mix all other ingredients except pecans. Pour liquids into dry mixture and mix just until moistened. Add pecans and mix well. Pour into 2 well greased and floured loaf pans. Bake at 325° for 1 to 1½ hours. Let cool before removing from pans.

STRAWBERRY BREAD

Susan Kurchinski

2 c. Florida STRAWBERRIES,
  mashed
1 c. sugar
½ c. shortening
1 egg

¼ c. buttermilk
1¾ c. all-purpose flour
1½ tsp. baking powder
1 tsp. baking soda
½ c. chopped nuts

In large bowl combine sugar, shortening, Florida strawberries, egg and buttermilk. Beat well. Add flour, baking powder, baking soda and salt; blend until mixed well, about 1 minute. Stir in nuts. Pour batter into

(continued)

greased loaf pan. Bake at 350° 45-55 minutes or until toothpick inserted comes out clean. Makes 1 loaf.

STRAWBERRY MUFFINS

Dee Dee Grooms

1 c. fresh STRAWBERRIES, stems removed	¾ c. sugar
	1 T. baking soda
1½ c. flour	¼ c. milk
½ c. chilled butter, cut into 6 pieces	2 T. sherry
	½ c. walnuts

Preheat oven to 350°. Put the flour, butter, sugar, soda and salt in the container of a food processor. Process for 10 seconds. In a small bowl, combine the eggs and milk. Beat well. Add egg/milk mixture to the other ingredients. Process 10-15 seconds. Add the sherry, then turn the processor on and off for a few seconds. Add the nuts and process for 10 seconds. Add the strawberries and process another 10 seconds. Bake in greased muffin pans for 18-20 minutes.

STRAWBERRY JAM BREAD

Linda Atkins

1 c. STRAWBERRY jam	1 c. butter or margarine
3 c. all-purpose flour	4 eggs
1 tsp. salt	1 tsp. lemon juice
¾ tsp. cream of tartar	½ c. buttermilk
½ tsp. soda	1 c. chopped nuts
1½ c. sugar	

Combine flour, salt, cream of tartar and soda; set aside. Combine sugar, butter vanilla and lemon juice in a soft ball. Drop onto wax paper and let it cool. Easy and foolproof.

STRAWBERRY NUT BREAD

Rose Peacock

2 pkg. (10-oz. each) sliced frozen STRAWBERRIES and juice	1 tsp. salt
	1 tsp. baking soda
	3 eggs, slightly beaten
3¼ c. flour	1 c. plus 2 T. oil
1¾ c. sugar	1¼ c. chopped walnuts
½ tsp. cinnamon	

Mix flour, sugar, cinnamon, salt and baking soda in a large bowl. Add eggs, oil, and sliced strawberries and juice, blend well. Do not use a mixer. Pour into 2 greased and floured loaf pans. Bake at 350° for 50-60 minutes.

34491B-00

STRAWBERRY HONEY BUTTER

FSGA Women's Committee

3½ c. whole fresh Florida
 STRAWBERRIES
½ c. honey

1 T. lemon juice
¾ c. butter

Purée the strawberries in the blender or food processor. Pour them into a saucepan with the honey, bring to a boil, and simmer over low heat 20 minutes, stirring from time to time. Stir in the lemon juice and chill the mixture. Have the butter at room temperature. Blend it into the strawberry honey mixture with a blender, food processor or electric mixer. Store in refrigerator. Yield: about 4 cups.

STRAWBERRY BUTTER

Jackie Perry

⅓ c. STRAWBERRY jam (freezer
 jam)
8 T. sweet unsalted butter,
 softened

½ tsp. fresh lemon juice
½ tsp. confectioners' sugar

Cream ingredients together. Allow to come to room temperature before serving. Refrigerate remaining portion. Keeps several weeks in the refrigerator. Yields: 1 cup.

STRAWBERRY BUTTER

Margaret Rodwell

1 c. STRAWBERRIES, washed
 and hulled
½ c. butter or margarine,
 softened

½ c. XXX sugar

In blender or processor, process till smooth.

DANA'S STRAWBERRY SHORTCUT

Dana Telese

1 qt. of fresh sliced
 STRAWBERRIES

1 ctn. of Cool Whip
1 pkg. of pound cake

Cut pound cake horizontally 2 times and alternate layers of pound cake, Cool Whip and strawberries.

STRAWBERRY PINWHEEL SHORTCAKE

Selma Gale

4 c. sliced Florida
  STRAWBERRIES
2-3 T. sugar
1½ c. all-purpose flour
1½ tsp. baking powder
½ tsp. salt

½ c. shortening
⅓ to ½ c. milk
1 T. butter, melted
⅓ c. brown sugar, packed
Whipped cream
Strawberry leaves, garnish

Combine sliced strawberries and 2-3 tablespoons sugar, stir gently and chill. Combine flour, baking powder and salt; cut in shortening with a pastry blender until mixture resembles coarse meal. Gradually add enough milk to form a soft dough stirring just until dry ingredients are moistened. Turn dough out onto a lightly floured surface. Knead 4-5 times; roll dough into an 11 x 8-inch rectangle. Combine butter and brown sugar; spread evenly over dough. Roll up jelly roll fashion starting at narrow edge. Pinch seams together, cut into 1-inch slices. Place on a lightly greased baking sheet. Bake at 425° for 18 minutes or until lightly browned. Serve with sliced strawberries and whipped cream. Garnish with strawberry leaves if desired. Yield: 8 servings.

BANANA BERRY NUT BREAD

FSGA Women's Committee

¾ c. mashed fresh
  STRAWBERRIES
1½ c. all-purpose flour
1 tsp. ground cinnamon
½ tsp. baking soda
½ tsp. salt
¼ tsp. ground nutmeg

2 eggs
1 c. sugar
¼ c. vegetable oil
½ c. mashed ripe banana, about
  1 large
½ to 1 c. chopped walnuts

In a bowl, combine the flour, cinnamon, baking soda, salt and nutmeg. In another bowl, beat eggs, sugar and oil until smooth; add the strawberries and banana, stir into the dry ingredients just until moistened. Fold in walnuts. Pour into greased 9 x 5 3-inch loaf pan. Bake at 350° for 60-65 minutes or until toothpick inserted near the center comes out clean. Cool for 10 minutes before removing from pan to a wire rack. Yield: 1 loaf, 16 slices.

MAKE AHEAD SHORTCAKE

FSGA Women's Committee

2 qt. fresh STRAWBERRIES,
  sliced
1 loaf (14-oz.) angel food cake,
  cut unto 1-inch slices
½ c. cold milk

1 pkg. (5.1-oz.) instant vanilla
  pudding mix
1 pt. vanilla ice cream, softened
1 pkg. (6-oz.) strawberry gelatin
1 c. boiling water

(continued)

34491B-00

Arrange cake slices in a single layer in an ungreased 9 x 13-inch dish. In a mixing bowl, beat milk and pudding mix for 2 minutes or until thickened; beat in ice cream. Pour over cake. Chill. In a bowl, dissolve gelatin in boiling water; stir in strawberries. Chill until partially set. Spoon over pudding mixture. Chill until firm. Garnish with additional fresh sliced strawberries if desired. Yield: 12 servings.

STRAWBERRY BREAD PUDDING

Reggie Gordon

2 pt. fresh STRAWBERRIES
1 c. sugar
$1/4$ tsp. cinnamon
Dash of cloves

12 slices day old bread
$1/3$ c. melted butter
2 c. sweetened whipped cream

Reserve several strawberries for garnish. Cut remaining strawberries in half; place in saucepan. Add sugar, spices and 2 tablespoons water; bring to a boil, stirring constantly. Reduce heat; simmer for 3 to 4 minutes. Remove crusts from bread: brush bread slices on both sides with butter. Line bottom and sides of $1\frac{1}{2}$ quart baking dish with bread slices; brush edges of bread with syrup from cooked strawberries. Alternate layers of cooked strawberries and remaining bread in baking dish; cover. Chill for several hours or overnight. Brush reserved strawberries with egg white; sprinkle lightly with additional sugar. Place on rack to dry. Garnish with whipped cream and frosted strawberries.

Recipe Favorites

Recipe Favorites

34491B-00

Cakes and Cookies

Strawberry Birthday Cake, page 38

Cakes, Cookies and Tortes

CAKES & COOKIES

DELIGHTFUL STRAWBERRY DESSERT

Kristie Gilford

1 qt. fresh STRAWBERRIES,
 sliced
3 egg whites
1½ c. sugar, divided
¾ tsp. cream of tartar

½ c. crushed Saltines
½ c. flaked coconut
½ c. chopped pecans
2 c. whipping cream
½ tsp. unflavored gelatin

In a mixing bowl, beat egg whites until soft peaks form. Gradually add 1 cup sugar and cream of tartar, beating until stiff peaks form. Gently fold in crumbs, coconut and pecans. Spread into bottom and up sides of a 9-inch pie plate. Bake at 375° for 20-22 minutes or until lightly browned. Cool completely. In a mixing bowl, beat cream, gelatin and remaining sugar until stiff peaks form. Fold in strawberries. Pour into shell. Refrigerate for 2 hours. Yield: 10-12 servings.

STRAWBERRY DESSERT

Linda Atkins

2 boxes frozen STRAWBERRIES
1 lg. round angel food cake, tear
 into med.-size pieces

2 sm. boxes instant vanilla
 pudding
8-oz. ctn. Cool Whip

Layer angel food cake in bottom of a 9 x 13-inch pan. Mix pudding according to directions and spread on top of layered cake for third layer. Thaw strawberries and mash with a fork. Spread over pudding, then cover with Cool Whip. Cover and refrigerate.

STRAWBERRY COCONUT CAKE

Linda Atkins

1 c. STRAWBERRIES, fresh
1 pkg. white cake mix
1 c. cooking oil
4 eggs

1 c. coconut
1 c. pecans
6-oz. pkg. strawberry Jello

Mix cake mix, oil, strawberries, coconut, pecans, eggs and Jello together, and beat with mixer at medium speed. Bake in 3 or 2 cake pans at 350° for 30 minutes. Frost with strawberry frosting.

Strawberry Frosting:

1 box powdered sugar
1 stick margarine
½ c. coconut
½ c. pecans

8-oz. pkg. cream cheese
½ c. fresh or frozen
 STRAWBERRIES, drained

(continued)

Cream sugar, margarine, strawberries and cream cheese together. Add coconut and pecan. Frost the strawberry cake after it has cooled.

STRAWBERRY CAKE

Gayle Gilford
Linda Atkins

½ c. fresh STRAWBERRIES or
 frozen STRAWBERRIES,
 thawed
1 white or yellow cake mix
¾ c. oil

1 pkg. strawberry Jello
½ c. water
4 eggs or egg substitute
4 T. flour

Mix cake, oil, Jello (dry), strawberries, water, eggs and flour together. Bake in 350° oven for 40-45 minutes. Makes 1 tube pan, or 3 layer cake or 1-2 layer cake or 9 x 13-inch pan. Cool and frost.

Frosting:

1 box confectioners' sugar
¾ stick of butter or margarine

⅓ c. fresh or frozen, thawed
 STRAWBERRIES

Mix sugar, butter and berries together. Spread on cooled cake.

STRAWBERRY SPONGE CAKE

FSGA Women's Committee

1¼ c. crushed Florida
 STRAWBERRIES
6 lady fingers or 1 sm. sponge
 cake

3 T. sugar
⅓ c. heavy cream
1 T. chopped nuts
¼ tsp. vanilla

Line spring form pan with split lady fingers or sliced sponge cake. Add sugar to strawberries. Whip cream with vanilla. Cover cake with strawberries and whipped cream. Repeat in layers until all material is used, saving part of cream for top of cake. Sprinkle with nuts. Chill 8 hours. Serves 2.

STRAWBERRY REFRIGERATOR CAKE

Rose Peacock

2 (10-oz.) pkg. frozen sliced
 STRAWBERRIES
1 (18.25-oz.) strawberry flavored
 cake mix
1 (4-serving size) pkg. vanilla
 instant pudding mix

1 c. milk
2 c. frozen whipped topping,
 thawed
Fresh STRAWBERRIES, for
 garnish

Prepare cake mix as directed on package. Allow to cool. Poke holes on top of cake. Purée thawed strawberries with juice in a blender or

(continued)

34491B-00

food processor and spoon over top of baked cake. Refrigerate at least 4 hours. To make topping, prepare pudding mix as directed on package using 1 cup of milk. Fold whipped topping into pudding mixture and spread over cake. Arrange fresh strawberries decoratively on top of cake and serve.

STRAWBERRY STACKS

FSGA Women's Committee

1 c. all-purpose flour
6 T. sugar
1 tsp. grated orange peel
¼ tsp. salt
¼ c. (½ stick) chilled unsalted
   butter, cut unto pieces

2 T. chilled solid vegetable
   shortening
1 T. orange juice

Whipping cream:

1 (1-pt.) basket
   STRAWBERRIES, hulled,
   quartered
1 T. Grand Mariner or other
   orange liqueur

1 c. chilled whipping cream
2 tsp. vanilla extract
4 sm. STRAWBERRIES

Mix flour, 2 tablespoons sugar, orange peel and salt in medium bowl. Add butter and shortening and rub in, using fingertips, until mixture resembles coarse meal. Sprinkle orange juice over. Stir with fork until moist clumps form. Gather dough into ball; flatten into disk. Wrap in plastic and refrigerate at least 30 minutes. (Can be made 2 days ahead. Keep chilled. Soften slightly at room temperature before rolling out.) Preheat oven at 375°. Butter heavy large baking sheet. Roll out dough on lightly floured surface to scant ¼-inch thick rounds. Re-roll scraps and cut out additional rounds, forming 8 total. Transfer rounds to prepared baking sheet. Brush lightly with cream. Sprinkle with 1 tablespoon sugar, dividing equally. Bake cookies until light golden brown, about 15 minutes. Cool on baking sheet on rack. Combine quartered strawberries, 2 tablespoons sugar and Grand Mariner in medium bowl. Beat 1 cup whipping cream, vanilla and remaining 1 tablespoon sugar in another medium bowl until soft peaks form. Place 1 cookie on each of 4 plates. Top cookie with berry mixture, dividing equally and allowing mixture to spill over sides of cookies. Spoon large dollops of whipping cream over. Top each with second cookie. Garnish tops with small dollops of whipped cream and whole strawberries. Serves 4.

PARKESDALE FARMS STRAWBERRY PECAN COOKIES

Parkesdale Farms

¾ c. STRAWBERRY purée, from
1 pt. STRAWBERRIES
1½ c. sugar
1 c. shortening
½ tsp. baking soda

2 lg. eggs, beaten
3 c. sifted flour
1 tsp. salt
¾ c. chopped pecans

Preheat oven to 350°. In large bowl of an electric mixer, cream sugar, shortening and baking soda; add eggs and strawberry purée. Mix just until blended. Stir in flour, salt and pecans. Mix well. Drop by rounded tablespoonfuls onto greased cookie sheets. Bake 15 minutes per pan. Makes 4 dozen. Nuts may be omitted if desired.

STRAWBERRY BIRTHDAY CAKE

FSGA Women's Committee

2 c. fresh Florida
  STRAWBERRIES, sweetened
1½ c. sugar
2¼ c. cake flour, sifted
2½ tsp. baking powder
½ tsp. salt

½ c. margarine
1 c. milk
1 tsp. vanilla
4 egg whites
1½ c. whipping cream

Preheat oven to 375°. Stem and slice strawberries, mix with ¼ cup sugar and refrigerate. Grease and flour a 9-inch round cake pan and a 9-inch diameter tube pan. Line pans with waxed paper. Sift together cake flour, baking powder and salt. Cream 1¼ cups sugar and the margarine until fluffy. Combine the milk and vanilla. Add dry ingredients to margarine mixture in thirds. Alternate with liquids, and stir until smooth after each addition. Whip the eggs until stiff, but not dry, and fold into batter. Fill pans ⅔ full, and bake at 375° for 25-30 minutes. Cool in pans for 10 minutes, then completely cool on racks. Enlarge center of tube layer to approximately 4 inches. Place solid layer on serving plate or tray. Spread 1 cup sliced berries on solid layer. Top with tub layer and refrigerate for at least 2 hours. Before serving, whip the cream. Add ¼ cup sugar and whip until very stiff. Fill center of cake with strawberries. Shape into a mound as high as possible. Frost cake with the cream mixture. Decorate with multicolored decorating candies, pink candles and strawberries. Yields: 8-10 servings.

STRAWBERRY CUP CAKES

FSGA Women's Committee

2 c. STRAWBERRIES, sugared
  (save juice)
1 box white cake mix

1 (6-oz.) pkg. strawberry Jello
½ c. oil
4 eggs

(continued)

38

Mix cake mix, oil and Jello. Add 1 egg at a time, beating well, then add strawberries. Beating well to blend. Bake in greased muffin tins to 400° oven until golden. Test with toothpick for doneness. Ice with strawberry icing. Yields approximately 24.

NANNY'S STRAWBERRY CAKE

Elizabeth McMullen

1 qt. fresh Florida
  STRAWBERRIES
1 box yellow cake mix

2½ pt. ctn. whipping cream
1 lg. box creamy white frosting
  mix or 2 sm.

Set aside ½ cup of the creamy white frosting mix. Stir whipping cream into the remaining frosting, mix (do not whip). Place in the refrigerator to chill preferably overnight. If you want to make it in one day, you can put it in the freezer. Bake cake as directed on box. Cool. Slice crosswise, making 4 layers. Use 2 (8 or 9-inch) cake pans. Remove frosting mix from refrigerator and whip until very thick, (like butter). Put a layer of cake, then a layer of frosting mix, then a thin layer of strawberries until you have used all 4 layers. Use plenty of frosting on each layer. For top layer, crush a few sweetened strawberries and use the juice to mix with ½ cup of frosting mix. Spread over tip layer and let drizzle down sides of cake. Garnish with 4 strawberries in center of cake.

STRAWBERRY JAM BARS

FSGA Women's Committee

1 jar homemade STRAWBERRY
  jam
3 c. flour
1 c. sugar
1 tsp. salt
1 tsp. baking powder

1 tsp. cinnamon
1 c. margarine
1 tsp. almond favoring
2 eggs, beaten
½ c. milk
Confectioners' sugar

Sift together flour, sugar, salt, baking powder, cinnamon. Cut in margarine; add almond flavoring, eggs and milk. Mix well. Spread ½ the batter in greased 9 x 18-inch pan. Spread with homemade jam; drop remaining batter by spoonfuls on top to cover jam. Bake at 400° for 30 minutes. Cool in pan. Cut in bars; sprinkle with confectioners' sugar.

STRAWBERRY ANGEL FOOD CAKE

FSGA Women's Committee

2 pt. fresh STRAWBERRIES,
  stemmed

1 angel food cake mix]
2 pkg. Dream Whip

Make angel food cake according to directions on box; bake in tube pan and cool completely. Insert strawberries into center of cooled cake

(continued)

by separating cake with fork. Continue around top of cake until all strawberries have been inserted into cake. Prepare Dream Whip according to directions on box. Frost cake with Dream Whip; allow to stand for at least 1 hour. Whipping cream may be used instead of Dream Whip.

STRAWBERRY HEAVEN CAKE

FSGA Women's Committee

1 qt. fresh STRAWBERRIES, chopped
1 (2-layer) pkg. butter recipe cake mix
1 (3-oz.) pkg. strawberry gelatin
1 c. boiling water
1 (14-oz.) can sweetened condensed milk
12-oz. whipped topping

Drain a small amount of strawberry juice for topping; set aside. Prepare and bake cake mix using package directions for 9 x 13-inch pan. Dissolve gelatin in boiling water in bowl. Add condensed milk and strawberries; mix well. Pierce holes in hot cake with handle of wooden spoon. Pour strawberry mixture over top of cake. Cool completely. Combine whipped topping with reserved strawberry juice in bowl. Spread over cooled cake. Chill for 2 hours to overnight.

HEAVENLY STRAWBERRY ANGEL CAKE

FSGA Women's Committee

1 c. heavy cream
2 c. sliced fresh STRAWBERRIES
1 pre-made angel food cake
1 T. drambuie
1/3 c. sugar

Whip heavy cream, drambuie and sugar together. Fold in sliced fresh strawberries. Fill center of angel food cake with cream mixture. Garnish with fresh berries. Serve chilled.

EASY STRAWBERRY CAKE

FSGA Women's Committee

2 pt. sliced STRAWBERRIES
1 lg. box strawberry Jello
1 med.-size Cool Whip
1 lg. angel food cake

Use pound cake pan. Tear 1/2 angel food cake into pieces. Put in cake pan. Mix Jello with 2 cups hot water. Mix strawberries with Jello mixture. Pour 1/2 mixture over cake. Spread 1/2 Cool Whip on cake. Tear other 1/2 of cake into pieces. Pour remainder of Jello mixture over cake. Refrigerate overnight. When ready to use put bake pan into hot water a few seconds. This will loosen cake. Turn out on plate; top with remainder of Cool Whip.

34491B-00

STRAWBERRY PECAN CAKE

FSGA Women's Committee

1 c. STRAWBERRIES
1 box white cake mix
1 sm. box strawberry Jello
1 c. oil

½ c. milk
4 eggs
1 c. coconut, opt.
1 c. pecans

Icing:

1 stick margarine
1 box confectioners' sugar
½ c. sliced STRAWBERRIES

½ c. pecans
½ c. coconut, opt.

Mix cake mix and dry Jello together, add oil, milk and eggs, one at a time. Mix according to cake mix directions. Add strawberries, coconut and pecans, mix well; bake in 3 layers at 350° for approximately 25-30 minutes or one 9 x 13-inch pan. Cool thoroughly before frosting. Cream sugar and margarine; add strawberries, pecans and coconut. Spread on cake.

FRESH STRAWBERRY CAKE

FSGA Women's Committee

2 pt. fresh STRAWBERRIES
1 yellow cake mix
1 jar strawberry glaze
1 (8 oz.) cream cheese

1 lg. Cool Whip
½ c. powdered sugar
½ c. white sugar

Bake cake as directed on box. Cut the 2 layers of cake with string to make 4 layers. Combine cream cheese, Cool Whip and both sugars. Set aside until cake is cooled. Wash strawberries and cut thin. Mix with glaze. Put a layer of cream cheese mixture, then a layer of strawberry glaze mixture. Alternate each. Keep in refrigerator.

LOW-FAT STRAWBERRY ANGEL DESSERT

FSGA Women's Committee

1½ pt. STRAWBERRIES
1 (6-oz.) pkg. strawberry gelatin
½ c. sugar

½ c. hot water
1 (10-inch) angel food cake
8 oz. whipped topping

Prepare gelatin using package directions. Stir in sugar, hot water and strawberries. Crumble angel food cake in 9 x 13-inch dish. Spread gelatin mixture over cake. Top with whipped topping. Chill overnight.

STRAWBERRY WALNUT TORTE

FSGA Women's Committee

1 pt. chopped STRAWBERRIES	1½ c. granulated sugar
1¼ c. flour	½ tsp. salt
⅓ c. powdered sugar	½ tsp. baking powder
½ c. butter	1 tsp. vanilla
¾ c. chopped walnuts or	2 T. cornstarch
pecans	1 T. lemon juice
2 eggs	Whipped cream

Combine 1 cup flour, powdered sugar, and butter; blend well. Press mixture into 9 x 13-inch pan. Bake at 350° for 15 minutes. Cool, drain strawberries; reserve liquid. Spoon strawberries over crust, sprinkle with walnuts. Beat eggs with 1 cup granulated sugar until light and fluffy. Add salt, remaining flour, baking powder and vanilla. Blend well. Pour over walnuts. Bake at 350° for 30-35 minutes until golden brown. cool; cut in squares. Combine ½ cup water, reserved liquid, remaining granulated sugar and cornstarch. Cook. Stirring constantly until thickened. Stir in lemon juice; Cool. Serve torte with sauce and whipped cream.

STRAWBERRY TORTE

FSGA Women's Committee

1 qt. fresh STRAWBERRIES	Sugar
1 pkg. white cake mix	½ tsp. nutmeg
2 eggs, separated	Few drops red food coloring
1½ tsp. almond extract	2 c. whipped cream
¼ tsp. cream of tartar	

Prepare cake mix according to package directions, using 2 egg yolks instead of egg whites and adding 1 teaspoon almond flavoring. Divide batter evenly among 3 waxed paper lined 9-inch cake pans; refrigerate. Beat egg whites with cream of tartar until frothy; gradually add 1 cup sugar, 2 tablespoons at a time, beating well after each addition. Beat until sugar is dissolved and stiff meringue is formed. Fold in nutmeg; spread evenly over tops of batter. Bake 325° for 40 minutes. Cool slightly; loosen edges and turn out of pans. Cool completely. Add remaining almond extract and food coloring whipped cream. Cut berries in half; sugar lightly. Spread small amount of whipped cream on top layer; add small amount of berries. Place next layer on top; repeat. Frost side of cake with whipped cream; make crown on top with small spoonfuls of whipped cream. Mound remaining berries in center of cake. May be frozen.

34491B-00

VERMONT STRAWBERRY SURPRISE CAKE

Elaine Harris

2 c. thinly sliced
  STRAWBERRIES
1 c. sifted cake flour
¼ c. granulated sugar
5 whole eggs, separated
1 tsp. lemon zest
1½ T. fresh lemon juice

2 T. water
¼ tsp. salt
¼ tsp. cream of tartar
¾ c. granulated sugar
½ c. Vermont maple syrup
1½ c. whipping cream
5 whole STRAWBERRIES

Sift together flour and ¼ cup of sugar. Beat egg yolks and lemon zest till thick and lemon colored. Gradually add lemon juice and water until thick and light. In another bowl beat egg whites and salt until foamy. Sprinkle in cream of tartar and beat until soft peaks from. Add ¾ cup sugar in 3 steps, beating well after each, fold in egg yolk mixture. Sift ¼ cup of flour over egg mixture, fold lightly, continue following flour by fourths until finished. Scrape batter into non greased tube pan. Bake at 375° for 30 minutes or until done. Remove from oven, invert pan. Let stand for 1 hour. Remove the cake from the pan. Cut crosswise through the center to make 2 rings. Pour ¼ cup of the maple syrup over 1 layer. Cover with sliced strawberries. Place second layer of cake over berries. Pour over remaining syrup. Cover with whipped cream. Garnish top of cake with whole fanned strawberries.

STRAWBERRY CAKE DELIGHT

FSGA Women's Committee

1 pt. washed and sliced Florida
  STRAWBERRIES
1 box yellow cake mix

1 lg. ctn. sour cream
1 c. sugar

Bake cake according to directions. Cool and split. Makes four layers. Mix and spread between layers of cooled cake the sour cream, sugar and strawberries. Freeze. Will keep up to six weeks.

STRAWBERRY FLAN CAKE

FSGA Women's Committee

1½ pt. fresh Florida
  STRAWBERRIES
½ c. milk
2 T. butter
2 eggs
1 c. sugar

½ tsp. vanilla extract
2 c. sifted flour
1 tsp. baking powder
¼ tsp. salt
1 pkg. strawberry glaze

Scald milk, add butter. Beat eggs in large bowl until light yellow in color. Add sugar and vanilla. Beating until light and fluffy. Sift together flour, baking powder and salt. Fold into egg mixture with hot milk mixture.

(continued)

Pour batter into greased, floured flan pan. Bake at 350° for 25 minutes or until cake tests done. Cool for 5 minutes and turn out on serving plate. Cool. Prepare 1 package strawberry glaze according to package direction. Fold into 1½ pint cleaned and drained fresh strawberries. Pour onto cooled flan and refrigerate until ready to serve. Decorate the edge with a ring of whipped cream. Makes 6 servings.

STRAWBERRY DREAM CAKE

FSGA Women's Committee

Crust:

½ roll refrigerator sugar cookies
½ c. pecans, chopped and
  lightly toasted

Filling:

¼ c. cold water
1 pkg. unflavored gelatin
10-oz. cream cheese, room
  temperature
3½-oz. marshmallow creme
3-oz. white chocolate melted
  and cooled to room
  temperature

2 c. Florida STRAWBERRIES,
  washed and chopped
8-oz. whipped topping

Frosting:

1 c. butter, room temperature
4 c. powdered sugar
3 egg yolks

1 tsp. vanilla
1-2 T. milk
4 oz. white chocolate, melted

Garnish:

Fresh Florida STRAWBERRIES

Crust: Freeze cookies for about 1 hour to ease preparation. Preheat oven to 375°. Spray bottom of a 9-inch springform pan with non stick spray. Cut cookies in slices about ⅛-inch thick. Cover bottom of pan with single layer of cookies, pressing together slightly to get complete coverage. Sprinkle with nuts, press gently into dough. Bake crust for 15-18 minutes until lightly browned. Allow to cool on wire rack but leave in spring form pan. **Filling:** Mix gelatin with water in a small saucepan over low heat until completely dissolved. Beat cream cheese until smooth. Slowly add the gelatin. Mix in marshmallow creme. Add melted white chocolate. Mix thoroughly. Purée strawberries and add to mixture. Fold in whipped topping. Pour into crust and refrigerate for at least 2 hours. **Frosting:** Cream butter until light and fluffy (6-7 minutes). Add powdered sugar a cup at a time mixing well after each addition. Add the egg yolks one at a time mixing well after each. Add vanilla and milk to make a good spreading consistency. Beat in melted white chocolate.

(continued)

34491B-00

Frost cake and decorate with fresh Florida strawberries. Yield: 10-12 slices.

LAYERED STRAWBERRY CAKE

FSGA Women's Committee

2 qt. fresh STRAWBERRIES,
  sliced
1 (18.5-oz.) pkg. butter recipe
  golden cake mix
2/3 c. buttermilk
1/2 c. butter or margarine,
  softened

3 lg. eggs
1/2 c. strawberry preserves,
  divided
2 c. whipping cream
3 T. powdered sugar
Garnish: fresh STRAWBERRIES

Beat cake mix, buttermilk, butter and eggs with an electric mixer until cake mix is moistened. Beat at medium speed 4 minutes. Pour batter into 2 greased and floured 9-inch round cake pans. Bake at 350° for 18-20 minutes or until a wooden pick inserted in center comes out clean. Cool on wire racks 10 minutes; remove from pans. Brush top of each layer with 2 tablespoons preserves. Cool completely on wire racks. Beat remaining preserves with whipping cream and powdered sugar at high speed with electric mixer until stiff peaks form. Place 1 cake layer on a serving plate. Arrange half of strawberries over layer; top with half of whipped cream mixture. Repeat procedure with remaining layer, strawberries and whipped cream mixture. Garnish if desired.

STRAWBERRY DESSERT

EvaNell Griffin

2 c. fresh STRAWBERRIES,
  sliced
1/4 c. firmly packed brown sugar
1/2 c. butter or margarine,
  softened
1 c. all-purpose flour
3/4 c. chopped pecans
2/3 c. milk

30 lg. marshmallows
1 (1.5-oz.) pkg. whipped topping
  mix
1 (3-oz.) pkg. strawberry
  flavored gelatin
1 c. boiling water
3/4 c. cold water

Cream brown sugar and butter until smooth. Add flour and stir until mixture resembles coarse crumbs. Add pecans. Press into a 9 x 13-inch pan. Bake at 350° for 15 minutes; cool. Combine milk and marshmallows; stir over low heat until marshmallows melt. Prepare whipped topping mix according to package directions and fold into marshmallow mixture. Pour over crumbs and chill. Dissolve gelatin in boiling water; stir in cold water. Chill until it reaches consistency of unbeaten egg white. Fold in sliced strawberries; pour over marshmallow layer. Chill until firm. Yield: 10-12 servings.

STRAWBERRY CREAM CHEESE DESSERT

EvaNell Griffin

9 whole fresh STRAWBERRIES
1½ c. graham cracker crumbs
½ c. butter or margarine, melted
3 T. sugar
½ c. chopped pecans
½ c. chopped almonds
1 (3-oz.) pkg. strawberry
  flavored gelatin

1 pt. fresh STRAWBERRIES
1 (8-oz.) pkg. cream cheese,
  softened
3 T. powdered sugar
1 (1.5-oz.) pkg. whipped topping
  mix

Combine graham cracker crumbs, butter, sugar and nuts; stir well. Press crumb mixture into an 8-inch square pan. Bake at 350° for 8-10 minutes or until light brown. Cool on wire rack. Prepare gelatin according to package directions; chill until it reaches consistency of unbeaten egg white. Remove stems from 1 pint strawberries; rinse and drain. Slice strawberries and stir into gelatin. Spoon gelatin mixture into crust; chill until firm. Combine cream cheese and powdered sugar; beat until light and fluffy. Prepare whipped topping mix according to package directions; add cream cheese mixture and beat until fluffy. Spread topping over strawberry filling. Chill several hours; cut into squares. Top each serving with a whole strawberry if desired.

STRAWBERRY EARTHQUAKE CAKE

Dee Dee Grooms

Fresh STRAWBERRIES
1 box white or yellow cake mix
8 oz. cream cheese

1¼ c. xxx sugar
Shredded coconut

Mix cake according to package directions. Grease and flour 9 x 13-inch cake pan. Layer approximately 1 cup or more of coconut on bottom of pan. Pour ½ of the mixed cake batter over the coconut. Cream together the cream cheese, xxx sugar and 1 cup mashed fresh strawberries. Drop cream cheese mixture in large dollops over cake mix. Pour remaining ½ of cake mix batter over top. Bake at 350° for 28-30 minutes. Do not over bake. Sweetened fresh strawberries can be poured over top of cake if desired.

34491B-00

STRAWBERRY TIRAMISU CAKE

Rose Peacock

Double Strawberry Sauce:

24-oz. ripe STRAWBERRIES, hulled, sliced, reserve 6 whole berries for garnish
1/2 c. strawberry jam
8-oz. cream cheese or mascarpone, softened

1/3 c. confectioners' sugar put 2 T. confectioners' sugar
6 T. Grand Marnier or orange juice
2 c. heavy whipping cream
1 angel food cake, 6-8 inches

To make the double strawberry sauce, purée 1 1/4 cup of the sliced strawberries with the strawberry jam. Refrigerate till serving time. Beat together the cream cheese, 1/3 cup confectioners' sugar, 1 teaspoon Grand Marnier until soft peaks form. Fold 1/2 cup of this into the cream cheese mixture. With a serrated knife, cut cake horizontally. Drizzle each layer with 1 tablespoon of the remaining liqueur. Spread bottom layer with 1/3 of the cream cheese filling; cover with 1/3 of the sliced strawberries. Top with middle cake layer. Spread with half of the remaining and sliced strawberries. Add remaining cake layer; top with remaining filling and sliced berries. Frost cake with remaining whipped cream. Refrigerate at least 2 hours or up to 24 hours before serving. Cut cake with a serrated knife. Serve each slice with sauce.

STRAWBERRY NUT CAKE

Erin Freel Best

Cake:

1 c. frozen STRAWBERRIES
1 box Duncan Hines white cake mix
1 box strawberry Jello
1 c. oil

4 eggs
1 c. flaked coconut
1 c. nuts, chopped, your choice
1/2 c. milk

Icing:

1 box powdered sugar
1 stick butter

1/2 c. nuts, chopped
1/2 c. coconut

Cake: Pour all dry ingredients into mixing bowl. Add milk, eggs and oil, mix until smooth. Bake at 350° in 3 (8-inch) baking pans for 25-30 minutes. Icing: Mix powdered sugar and butter together until blended; then add strawberries, nuts and coconut. Stir until well blended.

NO BAKE STRAWBERRY BOTTOM CHEESECAKE

Linda Atkins

1 pt. fresh STRAWBERRIES,
  sliced thinly
1 Keebler Ready Crust Graham
  cracker pie crust (6-oz.)
4 oz. cream cheese
¼ c. sugar

½ c. sour cream
1 tsp. vanilla
1 c. strawberry glaze
4 oz. frozen non-dairy whipped
  topping

Slice strawberries and place on paper towels to drain. Beat cream cheese until smooth. Gradually beat in sugar. Blend in sour cream and vanilla. Fold in whipped topping, blend well. Spread thin layer of glaze over bottom of crust. Place strawberry slices on glaze and cover with another thin layer of glaze. Gently spoon mixture over glazed berries in crust. Cover with inverted dome and chill until set, at least 4 hours. Store leftover pie in refrigerator.

Variation: For a plain no bake cheese cake, omit strawberries and glaze, double the amount of all the other ingredients. Preparation Time: 15 minutes. Chilling time: 4 plus hours.

CRESTED STRAWBERRY CAKE

Linda Atkins

1 pt. STRAWBERRIES
Warm, baked 8-inch layer of
  Duncan Hines Deluxe II yellow
  cake

4 T. sugar
½ pt. dairy sour cream

About an hour before serving time, wash and hull berries; cut them in half, if desired. Toss with 2 tablespoons sugar and let stand at room temperature. To serve, top warm, baked cake layer with the sweetened berries. Blend sour cream with 2 tablespoons sugar and spoon some over each serving. Frost the other layer, use it to make another dessert or freeze it.

JAM CAKE

Linda Atkins

1 c. STRAWBERRY jam
1 c. shortening
½ tsp. salt
2 c. sugar
1 tsp. soda

3 egg yolks, well beaten
3 c. flour
1 tsp. cinnamon
1 c. buttermilk
3 egg whites, beaten stiff

Cream together shortening and sugar. Add egg yolks and jam. Beat well. Mix flour, salt, soda and cinnamon together, add to shortening mixture alternately with buttermilk. Fold in egg whites last. Bake in

(continued)

34491B-00

3 (9-inch) layers at 350° for 30 minutes. Cool and frost with Mocha Chocolate Frosting.

Mocha Chocolate Frosting:

6 T. cocoa
6 T. hot coffee
6 T. butter

1 tsp. vanilla extract
3 c. confectioners' sugar

Mix cocoa, coffee, butter, vanilla and sugar together and frost cooled Jam cake layers.

RED, WHITE AND BLUEBERRY DELIGHT

Linda Atkins

1 pt. fresh STRAWBERRIES, sliced, drained well
1 can Eagle Brand sweetened condensed milk
1/3 c. Real Lemon reconstituted lemon juice
2 tsp. grated lemon rind

2 c. plain yogurt
1/2 c. chopped pecans
1 c. miniature white marshmallows
1 c. fresh or frozen blueberries, drained well

In large bowl, combine sweetened condensed milk, lemon juice and lemon peel. Mix well. Stir in yogurt, marshmallows and nuts. In a 9 x 13-inch pan or baking dish spread 1/2 the mixture. Arrange 1/2 the strawberries and blueberries on top. Cover with rest of sweetened condensed milk mixture and top with rest of fruit. Cover with foil; freeze until firm. Remove from freezer 10 minutes before cutting. Makes 15 servings.

NEAPOLITAN REFRIGERATOR SHEET CAKE

FSGA Women's Committee

1 pkg. (3-oz.) STRAWBERRY flavored gelatin

1 pkg. Duncan Hines Deluxe II Fudge Marble cake mix

Dissolve gelatin in 3/4 cup boiling water. Add 1/2 cup cold water; set aside at room temperature. Mix and bake cake as directed on package in a 9 x 13-inch pan. Cool cake 20-25 minutes. With cake still in the pan and warm, poke deep holes through top of cake with a meat fork or toothpick; space holes about 1 inch apart. With a cup slowly pour gelatin mixture over cake. Refrigerate cake while preparing topping.

Topping:

1 env. (1 1/2-oz.) whipped topping mix
1 pkg. (4-serving size) vanilla instant pudding and pie filling mix

1 1/2 c. cold milk
1 tsp. vanilla extract, if desired
Strawberry halves or slices, if desired

(continued)

Blend topping mix, instant pudding mix, cold milk and vanilla extract in a chilled deep bowl and beat until stiff and fluffy (3-8 minutes). Immediately frost cake with topping mixture. If desired garnish with strawberry halves or slices.

Note: Cake must be stored in refrigerator and served chilled. Makes 16-20 servings.

STRAWBERRY MERINGUE CAKE

FSGA Women's Committee

2 pt. fresh Florida
 STRAWBERRIES
1 (18-14-oz.) yellow cake mix
1⅓ c. orange juice
4 eggs, separated

1½ tsp. orange peel, grated
¼ tsp. cream of tartar
1 c. plus ¼ c. sugar
2 c. whipping cream

In a mixing bowl, combine cake mix, orange juice, egg yolks and orange peel. Beat on medium speed for 4 minutes. Pour into greased and floured 9-inch round baking pans; set aside. In a mixing bowl, beat egg whites and cream of tartar on medium until foamy. Gradually beat in 1 cup sugar a tablespoon at a time, on high until stiff glossy peaks form and sugar is dissolved. Spread the meringue evenly over cake batter. Bake at 350° for 35 minutes or until meringue is lightly browned. Cool in pans on wire racks (meringue will crack). Beat cream until stiff peaks form. Mash ½ cup Florida strawberries with remaining sugar; fold into whipped cream. Loosen edges of cakes from pans with a knife. Using 2 large spatulas carefully remove one cake to a serving platter meringue side up. Carefully spread ⅔ of the cream mixture. Repeat layers. Store in refrigerator. Yield: 12-16 servings.

STRAWBERRY MERINGUE TORTE

FSGA Women's Committee

1 qt. Florida STRAWBERRIES,
 sliced
¼ c. butter or margarine
½ c. sugar
2 eggs, separated
1¾ c. sifted cake flour
2 tsp. baking powder

Dash of salt
½ c. milk
¼ tsp. vanilla extract
¼ tsp. almond extract
½ c. sugar
¼-½ c. sugar

Cream softened butter; gradually add ½ cup sugar; beating well at medium speed. Add egg yolks one at a time, beating after each one. Combine flour, baking powder and salt; add to creamed mixture alternately with milk. Beginning and ending with flour mixture. Mixing well after each addition. Stir in vanilla and almond extract. Spoon batter into 2 greased and wax paper lined 8-inch cake pans. Set aside. Beat egg whites, (at room temperature) at high speed of an electric mixer 1

(continued)

34491B-00

minute. Gradually add ½ cup sugar, 1 tablespoon at a time; beating until soft peaks form and sugar dissolves. Spread ½ of meringue over cold batter of each pan. Bake at 350° for 25 minutes. Cool in pans 10 minutes; remove cake layers from pans. Remove wax paper and cool meringue side up on wire racks. Combine strawberries and ½ to ¼ cup sugar in a bowl. Place one cake layer meringue side up on serving plate. Spoon ½ mixture strawberries. Place second cake layer meringue side up spoon remaining strawberries over cake. Chill.

UPSIDE DOWN STRAWBERRY SHORTCAKE

FSGA Women's Committee

2 qt. Florida STRAWBERRIES
1 c. miniature marshmallows
1 (3-oz.) pkg. strawberry gelatin
½ c. shortening
1½ c. sugar
3 eggs
1 tsp. vanilla extract

2¼ c. all-purpose flour
3 tsp. baking powder
½ tsp. salt
1 c. milk
Fresh Florida STRAWBERRIES
  whole

Sprinkle marshmallows evenly into a greased 9 x 13-inch baking dish. Set aside. In a bowl slice strawberries, sweeten with sugar, ½ cup. Add gelatin; set aside. In a bowl, cream shortening and sugar. Add the eggs one at a time beating well after each addition. Beat in vanilla. Combine flour, baking powder and salt; add to creamed mixture alternately with milk. Pour batter over marshmallows. Spoon strawberry mixture evenly over batter. Bake at 350° for 45-50 minutes or until a toothpick inserted comes out clean. Cool on a wire rack. Garnish with whole Florida strawberries and whipped cream.

STRAWBERRY BANANA SPLIT CAKE

Kristie Gilford

Crust:

2 c. graham cracker crumbs
½ c. butter, melted

¼ c. sugar

Filling:

2 qt. fresh STRAWBERRIES,
  sliced
½ c. butter, softened
2 c. confectioners' sugar
1 T. milk

1 tsp. vanilla extract
3 lg. firm bananas, sliced
2 cans crushed pineapple,
  drained

Topping:

2 c. whipping cream
¼ c. confectioners' sugar

1½ c. chopped walnuts

(continued)

Combine crumbs, butter and sugar; press into ungreased 9 x 13-inch dish. Chill for 1 hour. In a mixing bowl, cream butter, confectioners' sugar, milk and vanilla. Spread over crust; chill for 30 minutes. Layer with bananas, pineapple and strawberries. In a small mixing bowl, beat cream until soft peaks form. Add confectioners' sugar, beat until stiff peaks form. Spread over fruit. Sprinkle with nuts, chill until serving. Yield: 12-15 servings.

FRESH FLORIDA STRAWBERRY CAKE

FSGA Women's Committee

1 c. crushed Florida
  STRAWBERRIES
1 pkg. yellow cake mix without
  pudding mix

1 pkg. strawberry gelatin
1/2 c. vegetable oil
1/4 c. water or berry juice
3 eggs

Frosting:

1/2 c. butter, softened
1 lb. powdered sugar

1/2 c. fresh crushed Florida
  STRAWBERRIES

Combine cake mix, strawberry gelatin, vegetable oil, water or berry juice and eggs in a large bowl. Mix with electric mixer. Stir in fresh strawberries. Pour into 2 greased and floured 9-inch cake pan. Bake 30-35 minutes at 350°. Cool before frosting. **Frosting:** Cream together butter and sugar. Stir in strawberries. Mix well. Spread on cool cake.

STRAWBERRY YUM YUM

Leota Mauersberg

2 pt. fresh STRAWBERRIES,
  sliced
1 c. plain flour
1 stick margarine, softened
1/2 c. chopped nuts

1 c. powder sugar
1 lg. Cool Whip
1 jar strawberry glaze
1 (8-oz.) cream cheese

Combine flour and margarine and press into 9 x 13-inch baking dish; sprinkle nuts over mixture. Bake at 350° for 15 minutes and cool. Combine sugar and cream cheese, add 1/2 container of Cool Whip. Then spread over cooled crust. Mix strawberries and glaze, then spoon over cream cheese mixture. Garnish with sliced strawberries or whole berries. Refrigerate and serve after chilled.

34491B-00

SUSAN'S STRAWBERRY PIZZA

Susan Kurchinski

5 c. Florida STRAWBERRIES,
  washed and sliced
3/4 c. chopped walnuts
1 1/2 c. self-rising flour
1 c. margarine, melted
1/4 c. brown sugar

8 oz. cream cheese
3/4 c. confectioners' sugar
3 oz. strawberry Jello
1 c. water
4 T. cornstarch
9 oz. Cool Whip topping

Crust:

Combine flour, walnuts, brown sugar and margarine. Press onto a round pizza pan and bake at 400° for 12-15 minutes. Allow to cool completely.

Filling:

Beat together 8 ounces cream cheese and confectioners' sugar. Fold in whipped topping and spread over crust.

Topping:

Mix together in a small saucepan strawberry gelatin and 1/2 cup water. In a separate bowl combine 1/3 cup water and 4 tablespoons cornstarch. Stir until dissolved and pour into gelatin mixture, stirring until thick. Add Florida strawberries and spread over filling. Can be served immediately or chilled.

STRAWBERRY COCONUT CAKE

Erin Freel Besst

1 c. fresh STRAWBERRIES
1 box strawberry supreme cake
  mix
1 sm. box strawberry gelatin
1 c. oil

1/2 c. milk
4 eggs
1 c. flaked coconut
1 c. chopped nuts

Frosting:

1 lb. powdered sugar
1 stick oleo
1/2 c. strawberries

1/2 c. chopped nuts
1/2 c. coconut

Combine all ingredients and mix well. Spread on cake

Blend milk and strawberries in blender. Mix with all other ingredients and bake at 350° in 3 (8-or 9-inch) pans for 25-30 minutes.

GORDON FAMILY CREAM CHEESE POUND CAKE WITH STRAWBERRY FROSTING

Erin Freel Best

Cake:

3 sticks butter
8 oz. cream cheese
3 c. sugar

3 c. sifted plain flour
6 eggs

Frosting:

1 lb. powdered sugar
1 stick oleo
1/2 c. STRAWBERRIES

1/2 c. chopped nuts
1/2 c. coconut

Cream butter and cream cheese, add sugar and eggs. Add flour, 1 cup at a time. Grease and flour tube pan. Bake at 325° for 1 hour. **Frosting:** Combine all ingredients and mix well.

PLANT CITY PARTY CAKE

Erin Freel Best

1 pt. STRAWBERRIES
1 pound cake
1/3 c. sugar

8-oz. cream cheese, softened
1 3/4 c. thawed Cool Whip

Cut pound cake horizontally into 3 layers. Crush 1 1/2 cups of the berries, reserving remaining berries for garnish. Add sugar to cream cheese, beating until smooth. Fold in Cool Whip, then crushed berries. Spread 3/4 cup between each cake layer and the remainder over top and sides of cake. Garnish with reserved berries and chill.

STRAWBERRY COOKIE PIZZA

Erin Freel Best

2 sm. pkg. frozen
  STRAWBERRIES, thawed
1 roll sugar cookie mix or other
  choice
8 oz. sour cream

8 oz. cream cheese
1 pkg. instant vanilla pudding
  mix
1 jar strawberry glaze

Pat out cookie mix thoroughly in bottom of rectangle cake pan. Bake cookie as directed, approximately 8-10 minutes. Cool before spreading next layer. Mix sour cream, cream cheese, pudding and sugar. Spread over baked cookie, layer thawed strawberries evenly over filling. Top with glaze and chill before serving.

54

34491B-00

STRAWBERRY UPSIDE DOWN CAKE

FSGA Women's Committee

1 c. crushed Florida
  STRAWBERRIES
1 c. sugar
2 T. butter, cut in squares
1 c. self-rising Flour

²/₃ c. sugar
¼ c. butter
½ c. milk
½ tsp. vanilla
1 egg

Place squares of butter in 8 x 12-inch baking pan. Mix 1 cup crushed strawberries with 1 cup sugar. Pour over butter. Set aside. Sift together flour, ²/₃ cup sugar, add ¼ cup butter, ¼ cup milk and vanilla. Beat 1 minute. Add rest of milk and egg. Beat 2 minutes. Pour over crushed strawberries and bake at 350° for 25-30 minutes. Cool and top with whipped cream and sliced strawberries.

FRESH FLORIDA STRAWBERRY COFFEE CAKE

FSGA Women's Committee

2 c. fresh Florida
  STRAWBERRIES, chopped
½ c. sugar
1 c. flour
2 tsp. baking powder

½ tsp. salt
½ c. milk
1 egg
2 T. melted butter

Combine sugar, flour, baking powder, salt, milk, egg and butter. Mix until just blended. Spread mixture in a greased 8-inch square pan. Arrange chopped strawberries over batter evenly. Make topping: ½ cup flour, ½ cup sugar, ¼ cup butter, melted, ¼ cup chopped nuts. Sprinkle over berries. Bake at 375° for 35-40 minutes. Serve warm.

SOUR CREAM STRAWBERRY CAKE

FSGA Women's Committee

3 c. fresh or frozen Florida
  STRAWBERRIES
1½ c. flour
½ c. sugar
½ c. butter
1½ tsp. baking powder

1 egg
1 tsp. vanilla
2 c. sour cream
2 egg yolks
½ c. sugar
1 tsp. vanilla

Combine flour, ½ cup sugar, butter, baking powder, egg and 1 teaspoon vanilla and mix well. Spread mixture into a buttered 9-inch or 10-inch springform pan. Sprinkle evenly strawberries. Combine sour cream, egg yolks, sugar and vanilla. Spread over strawberries. Bake at 350° for 1 hour.

FRESH STRAWBERRY CREAM TORTE

Erin Freel Best

Nut Crust:

½ c. pecans or walnuts
1½ c. flour

2 T. sugar
¾ c. butter

Filling:

1 (8-oz.) pkg. cream cheese
½ c. sugar

1 c. whipping cream
4 c. STRAWBERRY halves

Nut Crust: In a blender or food processor whirl ½ cup nuts to fine powder. Add flour and sugar. Add butter in chunks. Whirl until mixture holds together. Press dough over bottom and 1 inch up the sides of a 9-inch torte pan with removable rim. Bake in 325° oven until rich golden brown, about 45 minutes. Cool in pan. If made ahead, wrap air tight and keep until next day. **Filling:** Beat cream cheese and sugar at high speed until fluffy. Still beating add whipping cream slowly in a thin stream. (Mixture thins if added too fast.) Spread cream cheese mixture in crust. Mound strawberries on cream. Remove pan rim and serve. Serves 9-12.

FROZEN STRAWBERRY MERINGUE TORTE

Margaret Rodwell

2 c. sliced STRAWBERRIES
1 c. sugar
2 egg whites

1 T. lemon juice
1 tsp. vanilla
½ c. whipping cream

Place 2 cups strawberries in large bowl and add sugar, egg whites, lemon juice, vanilla. With electric mixer, blend on low speed until firm peaks form, 15 minutes. In another bowl, beat whipping cream until peaks form. Fold together with strawberry mixture. Pour into container and freeze until firm. To use small flower pots, place a small piece of aluminum foil on bottom of pot to cover hole. Place cut straw in center of pot and fill with mixture. Top with chocolate cookie crumbs. Freeze until firm. Before serving place flower into straw. The above recipe can also be poured into a baked graham cracker crust in a 10-inch spring form pan. After freezing remove from pan and decorate with 8 strawberries cut in half, around edge of torte and spoon with 2 cups of strawberries. Makes 8-10 servings.

STRAWBERRY CRISP

Glenda McNary

3 c. sliced fresh
  STRAWBERRIES
1 c. uncooked oatmeal
1 c. all-purpose flour

1 c. brown sugar
¼ c. chopped walnuts
½ c. butter
½ c. sugar

(continued)

34491B-00

Mix together oatmeal, flour and brown sugar. Add nuts. Cut in butter until crumbly. In another bowl, mix strawberries and white sugar together. Grease an 8-inch square pan. Spread half the crumb mixture on bottom. Cover with strawberries. Spread remaining crumb mixture over top. Bake at 350° for 45 minutes. Serve warm or cold with whipped cream or topping.

Recipe Favorites

Recipe Favorites

34491B-00

Winter Warmers

Strawberry Drizzle Pie, page 68

Pies, Cobblers, Tarts, Trifles and Custards

WINTER WARMERS

BANANA SPLIT PIE

FSGA Women's Committee

1 c. hot fudge sauce
1 (9-inch) chocolate cookie pie crust
1½ bananas, peeled and sliced
1 pt. vanilla ice cream, softened
1 (8-oz.) can crushed pineapple, drained

2 c. whipped cream, whipped to peaks with 2 T. powdered sugar
½ c. chopped walnuts

Spread hot fudge sauce over bottom of crust. Arrange bananas over. Spoon ice cream over. Cover and freeze 4 hours. (Can be prepared 1 day ahead.) Spoon pineapple over ice cream. Arrange strawberries over. Top with whipped cream. Sprinkle with nuts. Serve immediately, serves 6-8.

DOUBLE STRAWBERRY ICE CREAM PIE

FSGA Women's Committee

1 (16-oz.) pkg. frozen unsweetened STRAWBERRIES, thawed, undrained
1 c. graham cracker crumbs
6 T. (¾ stick) butter, melted
2 T. sugar
1 pt. strawberry ice cream, slightly softened

1 pt. vanilla ice cream, slightly softened
16 lg. marshmallows
2 egg whites, room temperature
¼ c. sugar
⅛ tsp. salt

Preheat oven to 400°. Combine graham cracker crumbs, butter and 2 tablespoons sugar and press into 9-inch diameter pie pan with 1½-inch high sides. Bake until edges begin to darken, about 8 minutes. Cool completely. Spoon strawberry ice cream evenly into crust. Freeze 25 minutes. Spread vanilla ice cream over. Cover tightly and freeze until firm, about 1 hour. (Can be prepared 1 week ahead.) Strain 2 table-spoons juice from strawberries. Stir marshmallows with juice in heavy small saucepan over low heat until melted. Cool completely. Meanwhile, beat whites in medium bowl to soft peaks. Gradually add ¼ cup sugar and salt and beat until stiff but not dry. Fold in cooled marshmallows. Spread over ice cream. Cover and freeze until ready to serve. (Can be prepared 1 day ahead. Refrigerate thawed berries.) Serve pie, topping each piece with spoonful of strawberries. Serves 8-10.

STRAWBERRY-CHOCOLATE D'LITE

FSGA Women's Committee

Crust:

2 c. chocolate cookies, crushed   ½ c. oleo, melted
¼ c. sugar

Filling:

2 c. STRAWBERRIES, sliced   1 pkg. (3-oz.) strawberry Jello
1 (8-oz.) ctn. frozen whipped   1¾ c. boiling water
   topping   1 T. lemon juice

Combine cookie crumbs, sugar and oleo. Press in bottom of 9 x 13-inch pan. Chill for about 15 minutes. In large bowl, dissolve gelatin in boiling water. Chill until thickened, but not set, about 30 minutes. Add lemon juice and beat until soft peaks form, about 5 minutes. Fold in whipped topping and strawberries. Pour into prepared cookie crust. Chill until set. Garnish with leftover topping and strawberries. Yields 12 servings.

ZUPPA INGLESE

Molly Freel Rowe

4 c. ripe STRAWBERRIES   Grated rind of ½ lemon
2 T. cornstarch   Pinch nutmeg
2½ c. milk   16 finger cookies
2 eggs, lightly beaten   Amaretto liqueur
2 T. sugar   ⅔ c. whipping cream

Mix the cornstarch with some of the milk. Beat the eggs, sugar, lemon rind, and nutmeg together and add the remaining milk. Mix with the cornstarch mixture in a heavy based pan and stir over a gentle heat until the mixture thickens and comes to a boil. Allow to boil 1 minute or until the mixture coats the back of a spoon. Place a sheet of parchment paper directly on top of the custard and allow it to cool slightly. Save 8 even sized strawberries for decoration and hull the remaining ones. Place half of the finger cookies in the bottom of a glass bowl and sprinkle with some amaretto. Cut the strawberries in half and place a layer on top of the finger cookies. Pour a layer of custard on top and repeat with the remaining cookies and sliced strawberries. Top with another layer of custard and allow to cool completely. Whip the cream and spread a thin layer over the top of the set custard. Put the remaining cream around the edge of dish and decorate with the reserved strawberries. Serve chilled.

    34491B-00

TIMMY'S FIREWORK TRIFLE

Erin Freel Best

1 pt. STRAWBERRIES
1 (4.6-oz.) pkg. vanilla pudding
   and pie filling mix, not instant
3 c. skim milk
1/3 c. sugar
1/4 c. orange juice
2 pt. blueberries
3 T. sugar

2 T. orange juice
1 (1-lb. 2.25-oz.) pkg. Pillsbury
   moist supreme white cake mix
1 1/4 c. water
1/4 c. oil
3 egg whites
1 c. whipping cream
2 T. powdered sugar

In medium saucepan combine pudding mix and milk. Prepare as directed on package. Cover; refrigerate until cool. Meanwhile, reserve 1/2 cup blueberries for garnish. In medium non metal bowl, combine remaining 2/3 cups blueberries, 1/3 cup sugar and 1/4 orange juice; stir to mix, crushing berries slightly. Set aside. Reserve 1/2 cup strawberries for garnish. In another medium non metal bowl, combine remaining 1 1/2 cups strawberries, 3 tablespoons sugar and 2 tablespoons orange juice; stir to mix crushing berries slightly. Set aside. Heat oven to 350°. Spray 2 (8-or 9-inch) round cake pans with non stick cooking spray. Prepare cake mix as directed on package using water, oil and egg whites. Pour batter evenly into sprayed pans. Bake at 350° for 30-40 minutes or until toothpick inserted in center comes out clean. Cool in pans on wire racks for 15 minutes. Remove cake from pans; cool 30 minutes or until completely cooled. Cut cakes in half horizontally to make 4 layers. Place 1 layer in bottom of clear 2 1/2-quart soufflé dish or glass trifle bowl trimming sides of cake to fit if necessary. Spread with half of crushed blueberry mixture; top with 1/3 of pudding. Top with second cake layer, trimmed if necessary, all of the crushed strawberry mixture and 1/3 of pudding. Top with third cake layer, trimmed if necessary, remaining crushed blueberry mixture and remaining pudding. Top with fourth cake layer. Cover; refrigerate at least 1 hour before serving. In medium bowl, whip cream until soft peaks form. Gradually add powdered sugar, beating until stiff peaks from. Top trifle with whipped cream. Sprinkle with reserved blueberries and strawberries. Store in refrigerator. Makes 12 servings.

TERRIFIC TRIFLE

Erin Freel Best

1 pt. fresh STRAWBERRIES,
   sliced or whole
1 (1 layer) box of yellow cake
   mix
1 box vanilla pudding

1 box frozen sliced berries in
   syrup
1 tsp. vanilla
1 (9-oz.) ctn. Cool Whip
1/2 c. slivered almond, opt.

Bake cake according to direction on box. Cool and cut in half horizontally. Put cake in a round deep clear bowl. Spread pudding on top of cake, then spoon thawed berries including juice over pudding. About every 2

(continued)

inches, pull pudding gently away from side of bowl so juice can run down and form design. Top berries with remaining cake layer. Mix Cool Whip and vanilla; spread over second cake layer. Place fresh berries on top along with almonds. Cover with foil and refrigerate 24 hours or overnight. Serves 10-12.

STRAWBERRY COOKIE TARTS

Selma Gale

1 pt. Florida STRAWBERRIES,
  sliced
1/3 c. shortening
1/3 c. sugar
1 egg
1 tsp. vanilla extract

1 c. all-purpose flour
1 tsp. baking powder
1/2 tsp. salt
1 egg white, slightly beaten
1/4 c. red currant jelly
2 tsp. water

Cream shortening; add sugar beating well. Add egg and vanilla and beat until blended. Combine flour, baking powder and salt; stir into creamed mixture mixing well. Chill. Roll dough into 1/8-inch thickness between 2 sheets of waxed paper. Cut dough with a 4 x 3-inch wedge shaped cookie cutter removing excess dough. Transfer cookies on wax paper to a baking sheet. Freeze 15 minutes. Remove cookies from wax paper and place on a lightly greased baking sheet. Repeat procedure with remaining dough. Brush cookies with beaten egg white. Bake at 375° for 10-12 minutes. Cool on wire racks. Combine red currant jelly and water in a small saucepan. Cook over low heat until jelly melts, stirring constantly. Cool slightly. Brush cookies with jelly mixture; arrange strawberry slices slightly overlapping on cookies. Brush strawberries with jelly mixture. Yield: 1 dozen.

STRAWBERRY-CHOCOLATE TRIFLE

FSGA Women's Committee

1 pt. Florida STRAWBERRIES
2/3 c. sugar, plus 1 T.
1/4 c. unsweetened cocoa
2 T. cornstarch
1/4 tsp. salt
2 c. milk

2 T. butter or margarine
1 tsp. rum flavoring
1 pkg. (3-oz.) lady fingers
1/4 c. apricot preserves
1/2 c. heavy cream

Combine in a small saucepan 2/3 cup sugar, cocoa, cornstarch and salt. Add gradually, the mix, mixing well until blended. Bring to a boil over medium heat, stirring occasionally. Boil for 1 minute, stirring constantly. Remove from heat. Add butter, stir until melted. Mix in rum flavoring. Set aside. Hull and slice strawberries. Spread cut side of lady fingers with preserves. Place one half of the lady fingers jam side up in a 1 1/2 quart glass bowl. Top with half at the pudding and 1/3 of the strawberries. Repeat layers with remaining lady fingers, pudding and 1/3 of the strawberries. Cover, refrigerate until chilled. Just before serving, beat cream

(continued)

                                                    34491B-00

along with 1 tablespoon sugar until stiff. Spread over strawberries. Top with remaining strawberries. Makes 6-8 servings.

STRAWBERRY DESSERT BERRY TRIFLE

FSGA Women's Committee

3 to 4 c. STRAWBERRIES
2 bananas, sliced

Angel food cake
Whipped cream

In the bottom of the trifle bowl, place 1½ to 2 cups strawberries. Tear angel food cake into bite-size pieces and layer on top of strawberries. Place sliced bananas on top of cake. Spread on a thin layer of whipped cream on top of bananas. Top with sliced strawberries. Garnish with dollops of whipped cream.

FLORIDA STRAWBERRY CHOCOLATE PIE

FSGA Women's Committee

1 pt. Florida STRAWBERRIES
1 pkg. (3⅝-oz.) chocolate
  pudding and pie filling
1½ c. milk
½ tsp. ground cinnamon
¼ tsp. almond extract

½ c. heavy whipping cream,
  whipped
1 (9-inch) graham cracker crust
¼ c. apricot jam
1 tsp. strawberry juice

Hull strawberries and cut in halves, set aside. Mix chocolate filling, milk and cinnamon in a medium saucepan. Cook over medium heat, stirring constantly until mixture comes to a full boil. Remove from heat, stir in almond extract. Cover with plastic wrap. Refrigerate until cool but not set, about 10 minutes. Fold in whipped cream. Pour into crust. Garnish with reserved strawberries. Chill until filling is firm. Combine in a small saucepan, the apricot jam and strawberry juice. Bring to a boil. Cool slightly then brush or spoon evenly over strawberries. Makes 6-8 servings.

QUICK STRAWBERRY COBBLER

FSGA Women's Committee

3 c. sliced Florida
  STRAWBERRIES
1 T. lemon juice
1 c. sifted flour

1 c. sugar
½ tsp. salt
1 beaten egg
1 T. butter, melted

Place strawberries in a deep baking dish. Sprinkle with lemon juice. Sift flour, sugar and salt then add beaten egg. Mix with fork until crumbly. Sprinkle evenly over strawberries, pour melted butter over the crumb mixture. Bake at 375° for 35-45 minutes or until crusty and brown. Serve warm with topping of cream, whipped topping or ice cream.

CREEPING CRUST STRAWBERRY COBBLER

FSGA Women's Committee

2 c. fresh Florida
  STRAWBERRIES, sliced
1/2 c. butter
1 c. flour

1 c. sugar
1 tsp. baking powder
1/2 c. milk
2 T. sugar

Melt butter in 10-inch baking dish in oven. Mix flour, 1 cup sugar and baking powder; stir in milk and mix until just blended. Spoon batter over melted butter. Heat berries with 2 tablespoons sugar just until hot. Pour over batter in baking dish. Bake at 350° for 30 minutes or until crust is golden. Serve warm.

STRAWBERRY CHIFFON PIE

Dana Telese

2 1/2 c. fresh STRAWBERRIES
3/4 c. sugar
1 T. lemon juice
1 env. unflavored gelatin
2/3 c. water

2 egg whites
1/2 c. whipping cream
Graham cracker crust
Whipped cream, opt.

Reserve a few strawberries for garnish. In a mixing bowl crush enough of the remaining strawberries with a potato masher, pastry blender, or fork to measure 1 1/4 cups. (Do not use a food processor or blender.) Stir in 1/4 cup sugar and the lemon juice, set aside. In a small saucepan stir together 1/4 cup sugar and the gelatin. Stir in the water. Cook and stir over low heat till sugar and gelatin dissolve. Remove from heat. Cool. Stir the cooled gelatin mixture into the strawberry mixture. Chill to the consistency of corn syrup, stirring occasionally (about 1 hour). Remove from the refrigerator (gelatin mixture will continue to set.) Immediately beat the egg whites with an electric mixer on high speed till soft peaks form (tips curl). Gradually add 1/4 cup sugar, beating till stiff peaks form (tips stand straight). When gelatin is partially set (the consistency of unbeaten egg whites) fold in the stiff beaten egg whites. Beat the 1/2 cup whipping cream till soft peaks form. Fold whipped cream into strawberry mixture. Chill till mixture Mound when spooned, (about 1 hour). Pile into graham cracker crust or baked pastry shell. Chill pie about 8 hours or till firm. Garnish with the reserved strawberries. Serve with additional whipped cream, if desired. Makes 8 servings.

34491B-00

STRAWBERRY CREAM TARTS

FSGA Women's Committee

1 pt. fresh Florida
  STRAWBERRIES
Pastry for pie shell, baked and
  cooled

Pastry Cream:

3 egg yolks, beaten
½ c. sugar
⅛ tsp. salt
2 T. flour

½ c. currant jelly

2 tsp. cornstarch
1 c. light cream
1 tsp. vanilla
¼ c. heavy cream

Pastry Cream: Combine egg yolks, sugar, salt, four, and cornstarch in top of double boiler. Gradually stir in light cream. Cook over boiling water, stirring constantly until mixture thickens and will pile up slightly when dropped from spoon. Remove from heat and stir in vanilla. Place waxed paper or Saran Wrap directly on top of mixture. Cool. When cold beat heavy cream until stiff. Fold into custard. Pour pastry cream into cooled pastry shell. Melt currant jelly over low heat. Place strawberries in pastry cream with pointed end up. Spoon currant jelly over berries. Refrigerate until time to serve.

STRAWBERRY SUGAR FREE ICE BOX PIES

Erin Freel Best

2 pt. STRAWBERRIES
4 T. sugar substitute
1 sm. box sugar free Jello
1 c. hot water
3 T. cornstarch

12-oz. prepared lite whipped
  topping
1 sm. ctn. lite whipped topping
2 (8-inch) graham cracker crusts
Red food coloring, opt.

Cut berries up in a large bowl. Use a 2-cup glass measuring cup and heat 1 cup water in microwave. Does not have to boil. Stir in Jello, add just a little cornstarch at a time and stir. (Cornstarch will lump if added all at once.) Pour Jello mixture over berries. Stir in 12 ounces topping and mix until there are no white spots. Add a few drops of red food coloring if you want a more "red" pie. Pour into 2 crusts. Divide the small container of topping in half and spread over top of pies. Garnish with half strawberries if desired.

STRAWBERRY SOUFFLÉ

Teresa Griffin

2 pt. STRAWBERRIES
Sugar
2 env. unflavored gelatin
4 tsp. lemon juice

6 egg whites at room
  temperature
¼ tsp. salt
2 c. heavy or whipping cream

(continued)

In a blender at medium speed, purée strawberries. In a 2-quart sauce-pan, stir ⅓ of berries and 3 tablespoons sugar. Sprinkle gelatin over mixture; let stand 1 minute to soften slightly. Cook over low heat, stirring until gelatin completely dissolves. Remove saucepan from heat; stir in lemon juice and remaining puréed strawberries. Pour mixture into bowl. Refrigerate, stirring occasionally, until mixture mounds slightly when dropped from a spoon, about 30 minutes. Prepare collar for 2-quart soufflé dish: From roll of waxed paper, tear off 26-inch strip; fold length-wise into 26 x 6-inch strip. Wrap waxed paper around outside of soufflé dish so collar stands about 3 inches above rim. Secure collar with cellophane tape. In large bowl, with mixer at high speed, beat egg whites and salt until soft peaks form; gradually spring in ⅓ cup sugar, 2 tablespoons at a time, beating until sugar completely dissolves and whites stand in stiff peaks. Using same beaters, beat chilled strawberry mixture until fluffy, about 2 minutes. In another small bowl using same beaters with mixer at medium speed, beat heavy cream until soft peaks form. Gently fold strawberry mixture and whipped cream into egg-white mixture. Spoon into soufflé dish. Refrigerate until set. To serve, remove collar from soufflé dish. Serves 12.

GRAND CHAMPION STRAWBERRY SOUFFLÉ

FSGA Women's Committee

6½ c. whole Florida
  STRAWBERRIES
2 env. unflavored gelatin
½ c. water
⅔ c. sugar
4 egg yolks, well beaten
½ tsp. salt

1 T. lemon juice
4 egg whites
½ c. sugar
1 c. whipping cream
Whipped cream and a few
  strawberries for garnish

Wash and hull strawberries. Purée them in a blender or food processor. In a saucepan, combine 1 cup of the purée, the gelatin, water, sugar, egg yolks, salt and lemon juice. Stir to soften the gelatin, then heat the mixture just to a boil. Cool, then refrigerate until mixture has the consistency of unbeaten egg whites, about 30 minutes. Meanwhile beat the egg whites until they form stiff, glossy peaks. Carefully beat in the ½ cup sugar. Whip the cream until it holds soft peaks. Fold the whipped cream into the egg whites, then fold the chilled berry mixture into the cream, egg white combination. Pour into an oiled 8 cup mold and chill at least 3 hours before serving. To serve, unmold onto a chilled plate and garnish with whole fresh berries and whipped cream.

34491B-00

MEGANS STRAWBERRY S'MORE TART

Megan Freel

Crust:

1 c. graham cracker crumbs
¹/₄ c. sugar

¹/₄ c. butter melted

Tart:

1¹/₂ c. thinly sliced
STRAWBERRIES
10 oz. semi-sweet chocolate,
chopped

²/₃ c. whipping cream
¹/₂ c. marshmallow creme
8 whole strawberries

Heat oven to 350°. In small bowl, combine all crust ingredients; mix well. Press mixture in bottom and up sides of 9-inch tart pan with removable bottom or 9-inch pie pan. (If using tart pan, place on cookie sheet for easier handling.) Bake at 350° for 10 minutes. Cool. Meanwhile, in a medium saucepan, heat whipping cream over low heat until bubbles from around edge of pan. Remove from heat; add chocolate and stir until melted. Cook 5 minutes or until luke warm. Place sliced strawberries in single layer in crust. Pour melted chocolate mixture over strawberries. Place marshmallow creme in microwave on medium for 30 seconds or until softened. Stir just until smooth. Quickly drop marshmallow creme by spoonfuls over chocolate layer. With top of knife, swirl marshmallow creme and chocolate to marble. Arrange 8 strawberries evenly around edge of tart. Refrigerate at least 30 minutes before serving to set chocolate.

STRAWBERRY CUSTARD PIE

FSGA Women's Committee

6 c. fresh STRAWBERRIES,
halved
1¹/₃ c. sugar, divided
6 T. cornstarch, divided
¹/₄ tsp. salt
2 c. milk
2 egg yolks, lightly beaten
1 T. butter or margarine

1 tsp. vanilla extract
1 baked (9-inch) pastry shell
1 c. water, divided
1 T. lemon juice
¹/₂ tsp. liquid red food coloring
Garnishes: sweet whipped
cream
Fresh strawberry

Combine ²/₃ cup sugar, 4 tablespoons cornstarch and salt in a saucepan, stir in milk. Bring to a boil over medium heat. Cook, stirring constantly, 1 minute. Whisk milk gradually into egg yolks until blended. Return mixture to saucepan. Cook over medium heat, whisking constantly, 1 minute or until thickened. Remove from heat; stir in butter and vanilla. Spoon hot filling into pastry shell. Stir together remaining ²/₃ cups sugar, remaining 2 tablespoons cornstarch and 2 tablespoons water. Bring remaining water to a boil in a medium saucepan. Whisk in sugar mixture; cook whisking constantly, 2 to 3 minutes or until thickened and clear.

(continued)

Remove from heat. Stir in lemon juice and food coloring; cool. Fold strawberries into syrup mixture. Spoon over custard mixture; chill 4 hours. Garnish if desired.

STRAWBERRY DRIZZLE PIE

Erin Freel Best

4 c. fresh Florida
 STRAWBERRIES
1 pie shell, baked and cooled
1(8-oz.) pkg. light cream cheese,
 softened
1/3 c. sugar

1/4 tsp. almond extract
1 c. whipping cream
1/2 c. semi sweet chocolate
 chips
1 T. shortening

Beat cream cheese until fluffy. Gradually add sugar and extract. Blend well. Whip whipping cream stiff then add. Place mixture in pie shell, starting at the outer edge, arrange strawberries pointing up on top of mixture. Melt chocolate and shortening together. Stir constantly until smooth. Pour chocolate mixture into a zip lock bag. Squeeze chocolate out of cut corner of bag to drizzle chocolate onto strawberries. Refrigerate. Serves 6-8.

STRAWBERRY TART

FSGA Women's Committee

1 1/2 pt. fresh STRAWBERRY
 halves
3 T. butter or margarine,
 softened
3 T. sugar divided
2 T. almond paste
1/4 tsp. grated lemon rind
1 lg. egg, separated
2/3 c. all-purpose flour

1/8 tsp. salt
1/2 c. milk
2 T. rum or 1/2 tsp. rum extract
2/3 c. whipping cream
1 T. powdered sugar
1 tsp. vanilla extract
Currant jelly glaze
Garnish: fresh mint leaves

Beat butter at medium speed with an electric mixer until creamy, add 1 tablespoon granulated sugar, almond paste, and lemon rind, beating well. Add egg white, and beat at high speed until smooth. Gradually add 2/3 cup flour, and beat until blended. Pat dough into 6-inch circle on a lightly greased baking sheet, lightly flattening top. Bake at 300° for 30-35 minutes or until lightly browned. Cool on pan on a wire rack 15 minutes. Remove from pan, and cool completely on wire rack. Whisk together the remaining 2 tablespoons granulated sugar, egg yolk, gelatin and flour, salt, milk and rum in a saucepan; cook over medium heat whisking constantly 3-5 minutes or until thickened. Cool slightly. Beat whipping cream at high speed with electric mixer until foamy; gradually add powdered sugar, beating until stiff peaks form. Whisk into gelatin mixture until blended; stir in vanilla. Spread over pastry. Chill 30 minutes

(continued)

34491B-00

until set. Arrange strawberries over filling; brush with currant jelly glaze. Garnish if desired.

THREE BERRY TART SHELL

Teresa Griffin

1¼ c. all-purpose flour	1 T. sugar
¼ c. shortening	3-4 T. cold water
4 T. cold butter	¼ tsp. salt

In medium size bowl, measure flour, shortening, butter, sugar and salt. With fingertips, blend mixture until it resembles coarse crumbs. Add cold water, 1 tablespoon at a time, mixing with fork after each additional until just moist enough to hold together. Shape pastry into ball; wrap and refrigerate 1 hour or until well chilled. Preheat oven to 425°. On floured surface with floured rolling pin, roll pastry into round about 1 inch larger than tart pan with removable bottom. Line pan with pastry, pressing pastry onto bottom and up side of pan; trim edge. With fork, prick pastry in many places. Line pastry with foil; bake 10 minutes. Remove foil; again prick pastry; bake 15 minutes or until golden if pastry puffs up, gently press it to pan with spoon. Cool tart shell in pan on wire rack.

THREE BERRY TART

Teresa Griffin

1½ pt. STRAWBERRIES, hulled	1 pt. raspberries
½ c. water	¼ c. red currant jelly
¼ c. sugar	1 tsp. lemon juice
1 env. unflavored gelatin	Tart shell, see recipe above, or
½ c. heavy or whipping cream	substitute graham cracker
1 pt. blueberries or blackberries	crust

Prepare and bake 10-inch tart shell as directed; cool. In blender at medium speed or in food processor with knife blade attached, blend 1 pint strawberries until smooth to make about 1½ cups purée. In 2-quart saucepan, stir water and sugar. Sprinkle gelatin evenly over mixture; let stand 1 minute to soften gelatin slightly. Cook over medium low heat, stirring occasionally until sugar and gelatin completely dissolve. Remove saucepan from heat; stir in strawberry purée. Refrigerate about 20-25 minutes, stirring occasionally, until mixture mounds slightly when dripped from a spoon. In a small bowl, with mixer at medium speed, beat heavy cream until soft peaks form. With rubber spatula or wire whisk, fold strawberry mixture into whipped cream. Evenly spread mixture into cooled tart shell. Refrigerate dessert 1 hour or until mixture is set. Slice remaining ½ pint strawberries. On strawberry layer in tart shell arrange blueberries, raspberries, and sliced strawberries. Prepare glaze: In small saucepan over low heat, heat currant jelly and lemon juice until jelly melts. Brush fruit with jelly mixture, refrigerate dessert

(continued)

about 15 minutes longer to set glaze (if fruit is placed on dessert too early fruit will become watery). Carefully remove side from pan and place dessert on serving plate.

STRAWBERRY-RHUBARB PIE

Faye Wetherington

1 pt. Florida STRAWBERRIES, halved (you can use frozen berries)	2 T. flour
	1 (9-inch) unbaked pie crust
	1 tsp. vanilla
1 egg	3 c. fresh rhubarb, cut into
1 c. sugar	½-inch pieces

In mixing bowl, beat egg, beat in sugar, flour and vanilla. Mix well. Gently fold in rhubarb and Florida strawberries. Pour into pie shell.

Topping:

¾ c. flour	½ c. quick cooking oats
½ c. packed brown sugar	½ c. margarine

For topping, combine flour, brown sugar, and oats in a small bowl; cut in margarine until crumbly. Sprinkle over fruit. Bake at 400° for 10 minutes. Reduce heat to 350°; bake for 35 minutes or until brown. Serves 8.

8 MINUTE LIGHT 'N FRUITY PIE

Charlene Shuman

Fruit, STRAWBERRIES	⅔ c. boiling water
1 pkg. (3-oz.) Jello gelatin, any flavor	2 c. ice cubes
	3½ c. or (8-oz.) ctn. Cool Whip

Completely dissolve gelatin in boiling water, stirring about 3 minutes. Add ice cubes and stir constantly until gelatin is thickened, about 2-3 minutes. Remove any unmelted ice. Using wire whip, (I didn't have one so I used mixer on low speed.) blend in whipped topping; then whip until smooth. Fold in fruit, if desired, Chill if necessary, mixture will mound. Spoon into pie crust. Chill 3 hours. Suggested fruits: Two cups diced peeled pitted fresh peaches or apricots. One cup fresh raspberries or blueberries, one cup strawberries or bananas.

34491B-00

MILE HIGH STRAWBERRY PIE

Nichelle Martin
Lynn Mobley

10-oz. fresh or frozen
 STRAWBERRIES
1 c. flour
$1/4$ c. brown sugar
$1/2$ c. chopped nuts
$1/2$ c. melted butter

2 egg whites
1 c. granulated sugar
2 T. lemon juice
$1/2$ pt. cream, whipped or (8-oz.)
 whipped topping

Preheat oven to 350°. Mix together flour, brown sugar nuts and butter. Place $2/3$ of mixture in the bottom of a 9 x 13-inch pan and save $1/3$ of the top. Bake for 20 minutes. Stir every 5 minutes. Prepare filling. Beat egg whites until stiff. Add strawberries, sugar and lemon juice to egg whites and beat for 10 minutes. Fold in whipped cream. Spread in pan and top with remaining $1/3$ of topping. Freeze.

RUBY RED STRAWBERRY PIE

Linda Atkins

1 pkg. (10-oz.) frozen sliced
 STRAWBERRIES, thawed
1 qt. fresh STRAWBERRIES,
 washed and hulled
$3/4$ c. sugar

1 (9-inch) baked pastry shell
3 T. cornstarch
Whipped cream, if desired
$1/2$ c. water

Combine sugar, cornstarch and water in large glass mixing bowl until smooth; stir in strawberries and juice. Microwave for 2 minutes on high. Stir and continue cooking for 2-5 minutes on high or until thickened (about 190°). Cool, fold whole strawberries into glaze mixture. Pour into baked pastry shell. Chill. Serve with whipped cream. Tip whole berries, point-up, for an easy cutting attractive pie.

STRAWBERRY ANGEL PIE

FSGA Women's Committee

1 c. Florida STRAWBERRIES,
 sliced
1 (3-oz.) pkg. strawberry gelatin
1 c. boiling water

$1/2$ c. cold water
1 (8-oz.) frozen whipped topping
1 (9-inch) graham cracker crust

Dissolve gelatin in water; add cold water stirring well. Chill until the consistency of unbeaten egg white. Fold in whipped topping and 1 cup strawberries. Spoon into graham cracker crust. Chill, 4 hours. Arrange additional strawberries on top of pie.

LEMON STRAWBERRY PIE

Dave Gale

2 c. sliced Florida
  STRAWBERRIES
1 c. sugar
2 T. plus 2 tsp. cornstarch
1 c. water
2 egg yolks, beaten
¼ c. butter

¼ c. plus 2 T. lemon juice
1 baked (9-inch) pie shell
2 (3 oz.) cream cheese, softened
¼ c. sifted powdered sugar
⅓ c. flaked coconut
¾ c. whipping cream
¼ c. toasted coconut

Combine 1 cup sugar and cornstarch in heavy saucepan; gradually stir in water, egg yolks, and butter. Cook over medium heat until mixture comes to a boil; cook 1 minute stirring constantly. Remove from heat and stir in lemon juice. Pour into cooled pastry shell. Cool. Arrange strawberries on top of filling. Combine cream cheese and powdered sugar beating until smooth. Fold ⅓ cup coconut and whipped cream into cream cheese mixture. Carefully spread over strawberries and sprinkle with ¼ cup toasted coconut. Cover and chill.

STRAWBERRY SUNSHINE PIE

FSGA Women's Committee

1 qt. fresh Florida
  STRAWBERRIES, sliced and
  sweetened with sugar

1 baked (9-inch) pastry shell
1 pt. lemon sherbet, softened
1 recipe meringue

Spread sherbet in bottom of pastry shell; freeze solid 4-5 hours. Prepare your meringue. Remove pie from freezer. Working quickly arrange strawberries over sherbet. Spread meringue over berries being careful to seal to edge of pastry. Place pie on cutting board; place in preheated 475° oven till golden. Serve immediately.

FRESH STRAWBERRY PIE

Gayle Gilford

2 c. sliced fresh
  STRAWBERRIES
1 c. water
2 T. Karo syrup

½ c. sugar
3 T. cornstarch
4 T. strawberry Jello

Cook water, Karo syrup, sugar and cornstarch until thick. Add strawberry Jello and sliced strawberries. Mix and pour into baked pie shell or graham cracker crust. Cool in icebox for 2 hours to set. Serve with whipped cream.

34491B-00

STRAWBERRY CHEESECAKE TRIFLE

Kristie Gilford

2 pt. fresh STRAWBERRIES,
  sliced
1 c. sugar, divided
2 pkgs. (8-oz.) cream cheese,
  softened
3 T. orange juice
3 c. whipping cream, whipped

1 loaf (10³/₄-oz.) frozen pound
  cake, thawed and cut into
  ¹/₂-inch cubes
3 squares (1-oz. each) semi-
  sweet chocolate, grated
Chocolate curls and additional
  strawberries, opt.

In a bowl, toss strawberries with ¹/₂ cup sugar; set aside. In a mixing bowl, beat cream cheese, orange juice and remaining sugar until smooth. Fold in the whipped cream; set aside. Drain strawberries, reserving juice; set the berries aside. Gently toss cake cubes with reserved juice. Place half of the cake in a 4-quart trifle dish or serving bowl. Top with a third of the cream cheese mixture, half of the strawberries and half of the grated chocolate. Repeat layers. Top with remaining cream cheese mixture. Garnish with chocolate curls and strawberries if desired. Cover and refrigerate at least 4 hours. Yield: 14-16 servings.

STRAWBERRY PINEAPPLE CREAM PIE

Dave Gale

3 c. Florida STRAWBERRIES
1 (3-oz.) pkg. vanilla pudding
  mix
1¹/₂ c. milk
1 (8³/₄-oz.) crushed pineapple
1 tsp. vanilla extract

¹/₂ c. whipping cream
1 (9-inch) pastry shell
¹/₂ c. water
¹/₄ c. sugar
2 tsp. cornstarch
Red food coloring

Bake 9-inch pastry shell, cool, set aside. Prepare vanilla pudding according to package directions using 1¹/₂ cups milk. Cool slightly without stirring. Fold in pineapple (drain pineapple well), vanilla and ¹/₂ cup whipping cream. Spread in cooled pastry shell. Chill till set. In small saucepan crush ¹/₂ cup Florida strawberries; add ¹/₂ cup water. Cook 2 minutes and sieve. Combine ¹/₄ cup sugar and cornstarch gradually stir into berries. Return mixture to saucepan and cook stirring constantly till thick and clear. Tint to desired color with food coloring. Slice 2¹/₂ cups fresh Florida strawberries in half lengthwise reserving a few whole "perfect" berries for center of pie. Arrange sliced berries over cream filling; spoon glaze over top. Chill several hours. Serve with whipped cream.

FRESH STRAWBERRY PIE

FSGA Women's Committee

6 c. fresh whole Florida
  STRAWBERRIES
½ c. sugar
1 T. lemon juice

1 T. cornstarch
1 (9-inch) baked pie shell
Whipped cream and whole
  STRAWBERRIES for garnish

Wash and hull the strawberries. Drain half of them on a towel. Purée the rest. (Strain through a sieve if you want a clearer glaze.) Combine the purée in a saucepan with the sugar, lemon juice and cornstarch. Cook and stir over medium heat until the mixture becomes clear and thick. Cool. Arrange the reserved strawberries in the pie shell and pour the glaze over all. Chill at least one hour before serving. Garnish with whipped cream and strawberries. Yield: 6-8 servings.

STRAWBERRY CHIFFON PIE

FSGA Women's Committee

1 c. Florida STRAWBERRY
  purée
1 env. unflavored gelatin
¼ c. cold water
3 egg yolks
½ c. granulated sugar
1 T. lemon juice

3 egg whites
¼ c. sugar
1 (9-inch) baked pie shell
Sweetened whipped cream and
  whole Florida STRAWBERRIES
  for garnish

Soften the gelatin in the cold water. In the top of a double boiler beat the egg yolks together with the sugar and lemon juice. Cook and stir over boiling water until the mixture thickens. Add the gelatin and stir until it dissolves. Remove from heat and stir in the strawberry purée. Chill about 30 minutes or until the mixture begins to set. Beat the egg whites until they hold stiff peaks. Then beat in the ¼ cup sugar, a little at a time, and continue beating until the egg whites are stiff and glossy. Fold the egg whites into the strawberry mixture and pour into the prepared pie shell. Chill at least 3 hours before serving. Garnish with whipped cream and strawberries.

BAKED STRAWBERRY PIE

FSGA Women's Committee

4 heaping cups of Florida
  STRAWBERRIES
Pastry for a double crust 9-inch
  pie

1 c. sugar
2 T. cornstarch
1 T. lemon juice
2 T. butter

Preheat oven to 450°. Wash and hull the strawberries and drain them on a towel. Stir together the sugar and cornstarch in a large bowl and mix in the berries. Sprinkle on the lemon juice. Let the berries stand

(continued)

34491B-00

for about 15 minutes. Line a 9-inch pie pan with pastry. Pour in the strawberry filling. Scatter slivers of butter on top and cover with a top crust. Seal the edges tightly. Prick a few holes in the center of the crust to allow the steam to escape, but don't make them too big or juice will run out. Bake 10 minutes in a 450° oven. Reduce heat to 350° and bake 40-45 minutes more or until crust is golden brown and the filling is thick and bubbling. Brush the top crust with milk once or twice during the last 15 minutes of baking. Remove from the oven and allow to cool at least 30 minutes before serving. The pie is good warm or cold.

STRAWBERRY LEMON TART

FSGA Women's Committee

3 c. sliced fresh Florida
  STRAWBERRIES
Pastry for a 9-inch pie
1/2 c. sugar
1 T. plus 1 tsp. cornstarch
1/2 c. water
3 T. lemon juice

1 egg yolk, beaten
2 T. butter or margarine
2 oz. cream cheese
1/4 c. sifted powdered sugar
1/3 c. flaked coconut
3/4 c. whipping cream
1/4 c. flaked coconut, toasted

Roll pastry into a 12-inch circle. Place in a 10-inch tart pan with removable bottom. Prick bottom of pastry with a fork. Bake at 450° 10-12 minutes or until browned. Set aside to cool. Combine 1/2 cup sugar and cornstarch in a heavy pan stirring well. Stir in water, lemon juice and egg yolk. Cook over medium heat stirring constantly until mixture boils. Boil 2 minutes or until temperature reaches 165°. Spoon mixture into prepared pastry shell. Top with sliced strawberries. Combine cream cheese and powdered sugar in a small bowl; beat at high speed of electric mixer until smooth. Stir in 1/3 cup coconut. Fold in whipped cream. Spread mixture evenly on strawberries and sprinkle with toasted coconut. Chill at least 4 hours.

FLORIDA STRAWBERRY TRIFLE

FSGA Women's Committee

2 c. whole Florida
  STRAWBERRIES
2 c. crushed Florida
  STRAWBERRIES

1 regular pound cake
1 pkg. instant vanilla pudding
2 c. milk
1 1/2 c. whipped topping

Cut cake into 12 slices, cut each slice in half (into 24 fingers). Using a medium glass bowl place 8 fingers on the bottom and the remaining fingers around the edge of the bowl. Top with crushed berries. Make up instant pudding, according to package directions and spoon over berries. Top with whipped topping and garnish with whole berries.

FLORIDA STRAWBERRY SUNDAE PIE

FSGA Women's Committee

4 c. chopped Florida
 STRAWBERRIES
1 baked pie shell
4 c. vanilla ice cream

½ c. sugar
2 T. cornstarch
2 T. lemon juice

Gently spread ice cream into pie shell or crust; freeze. **Sauce:** Crush ½ the berries, add sugar and cornstarch. Cook and stir over medium heat until mixture begins to thicken. Stir in lemon juice, continue cooking until thick and clear 3-4 minutes. Chill. Fold in remaining berries. Serve cold.

STRAWBERRY PETAL PIE

Selma Gale

1 pt. fresh Florida
 STRAWBERRIES, sliced
Pastry for 9-inch single crust
1 env. (1 T.) unflavored gelatin
¼ c. sugar
1 c. orange juice

2 T. lemon juice
3 egg yolks, slightly beaten
1 tsp. grated orange peel
3 egg whites
¼ c. sugar

Fit pastry into pie plate, trim even with edge. From remaining dough, cut 1-inch circles. Moisten rim of pie shell with water and place circles on rim, overlapping slightly. Press each circle with fork to seal in place. Prick well. Bake at 450° 10-12 minutes. Cool. Combine gelatin, sugar and dash of salt in saucepan; stir in orange and lemon juices, add egg yolks. Cook and stir over medium heat just until mixtures come to a boil. Remove from heat; add orange peel. Chill till partially set. Beat egg whites till soft peaks form; gradually add sugar; beating to stiff peaks. Fold in gelatin mixture. Spread half the filling in pastry shell. Top with 1 cup strawberries. Pile in remaining filling and top with remaining strawberries. Chill 2-3 hours. Serve with whipped cream.

STRAWBERRIES AND CREAM IN PHYLLO CUPS

Sue Harrell

1 pt. fresh STRAWBERRIES
1 T. granulated sugar
3 sheets frozen phyllo pastry,
 thawed
Butter flavored cooking spray

1 (3 oz.) cream cheese, softened
⅓ c. sour cream
¼ c. sifted confectioners' sugar
1 T. vanilla extract

Slice strawberries into a small bowl. Stir in granulated sugar; set aside. Preheat oven to 375°. Spray each sheet of pastry with cooking spray. Stack pastry sheets together; cut into thirds horizontally and vertically to make 9 rectangles (each small rectangle will have 3 layers of pastry).

(continued)

76

34491B-00

Arrange layers in each rectangle with points staggered. Place each set of pastry pieces in a muffin cup, sprayed with cooking spray. Bake 9-11 minutes or until lightly browned. Cool completely in pan. Transfer phyllo cups to a serving plate. In a small bowl, beat cream cheese, sour cream, confectioners' sugar, and vanilla until smooth. Spoon cream cheese mixture evenly into phyllo cups. Top with strawberries. Serve immediately.

STRAWBERRY-PINEAPPLE GLAZED PIE

FSGA Women's Committee

4 c. sliced STRAWBERRIES
1 pkg. pie crust mix or 2 crust
 pastry
8½-oz. can crushed pineapple,
 drained
¾ c. sugar

¼ c. cornstarch
2 T. lemon juice
½ tsp. salt
2 T. white corn syrup
Red food coloring

Make pie crust as directed on package. Roll out ¾ of the dough in circle about 1½-inch wider than inverted 9-inch pie plate. Roll out remaining pastry into 12 x 6-inch rectangle; cut into 8 strips, ½-inch wide. Combine strawberries, pineapple, sugar, cornstarch, lemon juice and salt. Pour into shell in pie plate. Make 4 designs on top of pie with pastry strips. Bake for 50 minutes in preheated 425° oven. Tint corn syrup with food coloring. Brush lightly over top of pie.

EASY STRAWBERRY PIE

FSGA Women's Committee

2 c. whole STRAWBERRIES
1 baked (9-inch) pie shell
¾ c. sugar
3 T. cornstarch
1 c. crushed strawberries

½ c. water
¼ tsp. salt
1 T. lemon juice
8 oz. whipped topping

Arrange whole strawberries in pie shell. Mix sugar and cornstarch in saucepan. Add crushed strawberries, water, salt and lemon juice. Cook for 8 minutes or until thickened and clear, stirring constantly. Let stand to cool; Pour over whole berries, spread with whipped topping.

STRAWBERRY-LEMON ICEBOX PIE

FSGA Women's Committee

1 pt. fresh STRAWBERRIES,
 sliced
½ c. lemon juice
1 tsp. grated lemon rind or ½
 tsp. lemon extract

1 can condensed sweetened
 milk
2 eggs, separated
1 baked 8-inch pie shell, chilled
4 T. sugar

(continued)

Combine lemon juice and lemon rind; gradually stir into milk. Add egg yolks; stir until well blended. Add strawberries; pour into crust. Beat egg whites until almost stiff but not dry; add sugar gradually. Pile lightly on pie filling. Bake in 325° oven for about 15 minutes until lightly browned. Cool and serve.

STRAWBERRY MARGARITA PIES

FSGA Women's Committee

2 c. fresh STRAWBERRIES
¼ c. sugar
¾ c. sweetened condensed milk
7 T. Tequila
6 T. Triple sec

1 T. lime juice
8-oz. whipped topping
2 (9-inch) graham cracker pie
  shells

Combine strawberries, sugar, condensed milk, Tequila, Triple sec and lime juice in blender container. Process until puréed. Pour into large bowl. Fold in whipped topping. Pour into pie shells. Freeze, covered overnight. May substitute 2 cups whipped cream for whipped topping.

STRAWBERRY PIES

FSGA Women's Committee

1 pt. sliced fresh
  STRAWBERRIES
1 (14-oz.) can sweetened
  condensed milk
¼ lemon juice

8 oz. whipped topping
1 c. chopped pecans
2 (9-inch) graham cracker pie
  crusts

Combine condensed milk and lemon juice in bowl; mix well. Stir in strawberries. Fold in whipped topping. Add pecans; mix well. Spoon into pie shells. Chill until serving time.

STRAWBERRY-TOPPED YOGURT PIE

FSGA Women's Committee

2 c. diced fresh
  STRAWBERRIES
1 pkg. (8-oz.) cream cheese,
  softened
⅔ c. plain yogurt

⅓ c. nonfat dry milk powder
⅓ c. honey
1 graham cracker crust (8-inch)
Orange peel strips, opt.

In a mixing bowl, beat cream cheese, yogurt, milk powder and honey. Spoon into crust. Cover and freeze for up to 1 month. Remove from the freezer 30 minutes before serving. Top with strawberries. Garnish with orange peel strips, if desired. Yield: 8 servings.

34491B-00

STRAWBERRY-CREAM CHEESE PIE

FSGA Women's Committee

1 pt. chopped STRAWBERRIES
16 oz. cream cheese, softened
1/4 c. sugar
1 tsp. vanilla extract

2 c. whipped topping
1 (9-inch) graham cracker pie
shell

Drain strawberries, reserving 1/4 cup juice. Beat cream cheese, reserved juice, strawberries, sugar and vanilla in bowl until smooth. Fold in whipped topping. Spoon into pie shell. Chill for several hours or overnight.

STRAWBERRY BRULEE

FSGA Women's Committee

4 c. fresh STRAWBERRIES,
halved
1/2 c. soft style or whipped
cream cheese

1/2 c. Dannon vanilla low fat
yogurt
3 T. packed brown sugar,
divided

Arrange strawberries evenly in bottom of shallow 8-inch round broiler-proof pan or 2-quart glass ceramic casserole. In small bowl beat cream cheese, yogurt and 1 tablespoon brown sugar with electric mixer until smooth. Spoon yogurt mixture over fruit. Top with remaining 2 tablespoons brown sugar. Broil 4-5 inches from heat 2-3 minutes or just until brown sugar melts and starts to darken. Serve immediately. Serves 4.

FRESH STRAWBERRY CRACKER PIE

FSGA Women's Committee

STRAWBERRIES, sweetened
3 egg whites
1 c. sugar
1 tsp. vanilla

23 Ritz crackers
1 c. chopped pecans
Whipped cream

Beat egg whites until stiff; gradually add sugar continuing to beat. Add vanilla. Have crackers mashed. Combine crackers and chopped pecans. Fold this into egg white mixture. Pour into well buttered Pyrex dish. Smooth out to form pie shell. Bake at 350° for 30 minutes or until done. Let cool; top with whipped cream and fresh sweetened strawberries.

Recipe Favorites

34491B-00

Cold Treats

Strawberry Longshore, page 82

Parfaits, Sundaes, Ice Cream and Sorbet

COLD TREATS

RED, WHITE AND BLUEBERRY SUNDAES

FSGA Women's Committee

1⅓ c. sliced, hulled
STRAWBERRIES
1 c. orange juice
7 T. Grand Mariner or other
orange liqueur
6 T. sugar
5 T. unsalted butter

2 nectarines, halved, pitted, cut
into ½-inch wedges
1⅓ c. blueberries
1½ pt. (about) vanilla ice cream
or frozen yogurt
Mint leaves

Combine orange juice, Grand Mariner, sugar and butter in heavy large skillet. Stir over medium-high heat until sugar dissolves and sauce comes to simmer. Simmer until sauce thickens slightly and is reduced to 1 cup, about 10 minutes. (Sauce can be prepared 1 day ahead, cover and refrigerate, bring sauce to simmer before continuing.) Add nectarines to sauce and toss until heated through, about 2 minutes. Add blueberries and strawberries; toss until heated through, about 1 minute. Divide fruit mixture among 6 dessert bowls. Place 1 scoop ice cream in center of fruit. Garnish with mint.

STRAWBERRY POPSICLES

1 c. STRAWBERRIES, puréed
½ c. water
1 env. gelatin, unflavored

1¼ c. sugar
1 tsp. lemon juice
1 c. fruit juice, boiling

Combine water and gelatin in medium saucepan; let stand 1 minute. Add hot juice, (may prefer orange or pineapple juice). Stir until gelatin is completely dissolved. Stir in remaining ingredients. Pour in popsicle molds or small paper cups; freeze until partially frozen, about 30 minutes. Insert ice cream sticks, and freeze until firm. Yields: about 6 popsicle.

STRAWBERRY SICLES

FSGA Women's Committee

1 (10-oz.) pkg. frozen sliced
STRAWBERRIES and juice,
thawed

¼ c. sour cream

Mix ingredients together, pour into popsicle tubs and freeze. Makes 6 popsicles.

STRAWBERRY SUNDAE CRUNCH

FSGA Women's Committee

1 (10-oz.) box frozen
  STRAWBERRIES
1 pt. fresh STRAWBERRIES
2½ c. Rice Krispies
1 can flaked coconut
1 c. chopped pecans
1 stick oleo, melted

¾ c. brown sugar
3 egg whites
1 c. sugar
2 T. lemon juice
1 lg. Cool Whip
½ gal. strawberry ice cream

Place Rice Krispies, coconut, pecans and oleo on cookie sheet and toast in 300° oven for 30 minutes, stirring every 5 minutes. Remove from oven and add brown sugar and stir until sugar is melted. Mix together 3 egg whites, sugar, lemon juice and frozen strawberries. Beat on high for 20 minutes. Makes a large amount. Add 1 pint fresh strawberries, sliced small and Cool Whip. Put half of toasted mixture in bottom of large, deep Pyrex dish. Pour strawberry mixture over mix. Slice ice cream and place over strawberry mixture until smooth. Add rest of toasted mixture over ice cream; freeze.

STRAWBERRY MILK MALLOBET

FSGA Women's Committee

¾ c. crushed, fresh
  STRAWBERRIES
16 lg. marshmallows

1 c. milk, chilled
1 T. lemon juice

Heat marshmallows and 2 tablespoons milk in top of a double boiler. Stir carefully until marshmallows are about half melted. Remove from heat and continue stirring until the mixture is smooth and spongy. Cool to lukewarm and then blend in remaining milk, crushed strawberries, and lemon juice. Pour into freezing trays of refrigerator and freeze, stirring several times. Serves 4.

STRAWBERRY LONGSHORE

FSGA Women's Committee

1 pt. Florida STRAWBERRIES,
  sliced
1 (8-oz.) ctn. whipped cream
1 (3-oz.) pkg. cream cheese,
  softened

1 pound cake, broken into
  pieces
Chocolate syrup
Caramel syrup
Sliced bananas

Blend whipped cream and cream cheese together until thoroughly mixed. Place a layer of pound cake in a 9-inch pan. Add a layer of sliced strawberries. Add a layer of sliced bananas. Top with a portion of cream cheese mixture. Repeat layering process. Chill. Spoon until

(continued)

dessert cups or glasses. Top with hot chocolate and caramel syrup. Add pecan pieces. Yield: 6-8 servings.

STRAWBERRY 'NILLA-WAFER PUDDING

FSGA Women's Committee

1 qt. STRAWBERRIES, sliced	1 ctn. whipped topping
1 box vanilla wafers, crushed	
1 pkg. vanilla pudding, prepare	
by directions	

Place ½ of wafer crumbs in deep pie plate, slightly oiled. Pour vanilla pudding mixture over crumbs, then place sliced strawberries that have been sugared with about 2 tablespoons. Top with remaining wafer crumbs. Chill overnight.

FROZEN LIME & STRAWBERRY CREAM

Molly Freel Rowe

1 c. STRAWBERRIES	3 egg whites
Juice and zested rind of 4 limes	1¼ c. whipped cream
1 c. sugar	

Measure the lime juice and make up to ⅓ cup with water if necessary. Combine with the sugar in a heavy based pan and bring to a boil slowly to dissolve the sugar. When the mixture forms a clear syrup, boil rapidly to 248° on a candy thermometer. Meanwhile, combine the strawberries with 4 tablespoons water in a small saucepan. Bring to the boil and then simmer, covered until very soft. Purée, then sieve to remove the seed. Whisk the egg whites until soft but not dry and then pour on the hot sugar syrup in a steady stream, whisking constantly. Add the lime and rind and allow the meringue to cool. When cold, fold in the whipped cream. Add the purée and marble through the mixture with a spatula. Do not over fold. Pour the mixture into a lightly oiled mold or bowl and freeze until firm. Leave in the refrigerator 30 minutes before serving or dip the mold in hot water for about 10 seconds. Place a plate over the bottom of the mold, invert and shake to unmold. Garnish with extra whipped cream and lime slices.

STRAWBERRY GRANITA

Teresa Griffin

2 pt. STRAWBERRIES, puréed	½ c. sugar
6 lg. whole STRAWBERRIES	1 T. lemon juice
1 c. water	

In 2-quart saucepan over high heat, heat water and sugar to boiling. Reduce heat to medium; cook 5 minutes. Stir in strawberries and lemon

(continued)

juice pour in a 8 x 8-inch baking pan. Cover with foil or plastic wrap; freeze, stirring occasionally until firm, about 5 hours. To serve, let granita stand at room temperature 15 minutes to soften slightly. Then with spoon or ice cream scoop scrape across surface of granita to create pebble texture; spoon into bowls. Garnish with remaining berries. Serves 6.

FROSTY STRAWBERRY SQUARES

Margaret Rodwell

1 (10-oz.) pkg. frozen
  STRAWBERRIES or 2 c. fresh
1 c. flour
1/4 c. packed brown sugar
1/2 c. chopped walnuts

1/2 c. butter, melted
2 egg whites
3/4 c. sugar
2 T. lemon juice
1 c. whip cream, whipped

In a bowl stir together flour, brown sugar, walnuts and butter. Spread in 9 x 13-inch pan. Bake at 350° 20 minutes, stir occasionally. Cool. Sprinkle 2/3 baked mixture in bottom of same pan. Save remaining. In large bowl combine egg whites, sugar, strawberries, and lemon juice; beat at low speed until mixture begins to thicken about 2 minutes then beat at high speed until stiff peaks form. Fold in whip cream. Spoon over mixture in pan; top with reserved mixture. Freeze 6 hours or overnight. Cut in squares.

STRAWBERRY-MARGARITA SORBET

FSGA Women's Committee

4 c. fresh Florida
  STRAWBERRIES
6 Florida STRAWBERRIES,
  whole, garnish
2 c. water

1 c. sugar
1/2 c. lime juice
1/4 c. plus 2 T. tequila
1/4 c. triple sec

Combine water and sugar in a small saucepan; bring to a boil; stirring constantly until sugar dissolves. Cool completely. Purée 4 cups Florida strawberries. Combine berries, sugar, syrup, lime juice, tequila and triple sec, stirring well. Pour mixture into freezer can of a 6-cup electric ice cream freezer. Freeze according to manufacturer's instructions. Garnish each serving with a fresh strawberry. Yield: 6 cups.

FROZEN BERRY SQUARES

FSGA Women's Committee

2 c. fresh BERRIES
1 1/2 c. graham cracker crumbs
1/3 c. butter
2 T. sugar

2 egg whites
1 T. lemon juice
1 1/3 c. sugar
1 c. whipped cream

(continued)

34491B-00

Day ahead: Combine graham cracker crumbs, butter and 2 tablespoons sugar together and press into a 9-inch square pan. Bake 8 minutes at 375°. Beat egg whites (at room temperature) and lemon juice until soft peaks form. Gradually add 1⅓ cup sugar, 1 tablespoon at a time and keep beating until mixture is fluffy. Fold in whipped cream and berries. Turn into crust. Freeze overnight. Garnish with fresh berries.

BREAKFAST PARFAIT

Teresa Griffin

½ c. sliced STRAWBERRIES
½ c. granola
¼ c. plain nonfat yogurt or
   cottage cheese

½ ripe banana, sliced
½ c. blueberries, or raspberries

Place half of granola in parfait glass bowl. Top with half of yogurt. Spoon half of strawberries over yogurt. Top with banana and blueberries, remaining granola, yogurt and strawberries. Makes 1 serving.

FROSTY STRAWBERRY CREAM

Erin Freel Best

1 (10-oz.) pkg. STRAWBERRIES,
   partially frozen
½ c. melted butter or margarine
1 c. sifted flour
¼ c. nuts, chopped
2 egg whites

⅔ c. sugar
1 c. whipping cream or Rich
   Whip or Pet milk, chilled and
   whipped
2 T. lemon juice

Stir melted butter, flour and nuts together. Place in shallow pan and bake at 325° until brown, stirring often approximately 20 minutes. Sprinkle ⅔ cup of this mixture in 9 x 13-inch pan, reserving remaining crumbs for top. Beat egg whites and sugar until stiff. In separate bowl, beat cream and strawberries 15-20 minutes at high speed, adding lemon juice. Fold into egg white mixture. Pour over crumb mixture and sprinkle remaining crumbs on top. Freeze for 6 hours. Cut in squares and garnish with fresh strawberries dipped in sugar.

FRESH STRAWBERRY SORBET

Erin Freel Best

30 hulled ripe STRAWBERRIES
⅔ c. sugar
¼ c. fresh lemon juice

⅓ c. heavy or whipping cream
2 T. framboise liqueur, opt. it
   will make sorbet a little softer

Place the strawberries, sugar and lemon juice in a food processor fitted with a steel blade and process until smooth. Pour in the cream and liqueur and process until blended. Freeze in an ice cream maker follow-

(continued)

ing manufactures instructions. Makes 1 pint or enough for 6 small servings.

DELILA'S STRAWBERRY SURPRISE

Erin Freel Best

1 c. sliced fresh
  STRAWBERRIES
1 c. butter at room temperature
½ c. brown sugar
2 c. flour

1 c. chopped nuts
1 pt. vanilla ice cream, slightly
  softened
1 tsp. vanilla extract

Preheat oven to 400°. Lightly grease 9 x 13-inch baking pan. Stir together butter, sugar, flour and nuts in large bowl. Mix very well with wooden spoon or your hands. Spoon loose mixture into baking pan. Bake for 15 minutes, stirring occasionally. When it is brown, remove from oven. Press half of the loose mixture into the baking pan and save the rest for a topping. In another bowl, combine softened ice cream with strawberries and vanilla. Pour this mixture over the crust. Sprinkle evenly with remaining crumbs. Cover lightly with plastic wrap and freeze for several hours or overnight. Remove from freezer 10-15 minutes before serving. Cut in wedges. Serves 10-12.

STRAWBERRY BREAKFAST SUNDAE

Nichelle Martin
Lynn Mobley

4 c. STRAWBERRIES
2 c. favorite granola

4 c. favorite yogurt

Layer ½ granola, 1 cup yogurt and 1 cup sliced, fresh strawberries in 4 parfait glasses. Serves 4.

HOMEMADE STRAWBERRY ICE CREAM

Gayle Gilford

2 c. STRAWBERRIES,
  sweetened to taste
1 can condensed milk, fat free is
  fine
1 sm. can evaporated milk, fat
  free and lg. can okay

1 c. sugar
2 tsp. vanilla
Juice of 1 lemon
Dash of salt
1½ qt. milk, skim okay

Mix condensed milk, evaporated milk, sugar, vanilla, lemon juice, salt, strawberries and milk well. Pour into churn and if needed add more milk to fill churn to proper level. Follow directions for your ice cream freezer.

34491B-00

STRAWBERRY RICOTTA CUSTARD

FSGA Women's Committee

1½ c. fresh Florida
 STRAWBERRIES
½ c. Florida STRAWBERRIES
 for garnish
2 c. ricotta cheese

¼ c. milk
4 eggs
¼ c. honey
2 T. cornstarch
½ tsp. vanilla extract

In the blender or food processor beat together the ricotta, milk, eggs and honey. Mash a few of the strawberries together with the cornstarch until it dissolves. Put the cornstarch mixture and the rest of the 1½ cups of strawberries into the food processor with the cheese. Blend until smooth. Blend in vanilla. Butter a 6-cup baking dish and dust it with granulated sugar. Pour the strawberry cheese mixture into the dish and place in a shallow pan of hot water. Bake in a preheated about 1 hour or until the custard is barely baked through. A knife inserted near the center should come out nearly clean. The center may still be slightly soft but it will set as it cools. Over baking will make custard coarse and watery. Remove the dish from the hot water and cool to room temperature before serving. It is good chilled too. It you are using the strawberry garnish, mix the remaining berries in the blender or food processor and pour over the wedges of custard like a sauce.

BAKED STRAWBERRY CUSTARD

FSGA Women's Committee

2 c. whole Florida
 STRAWBERRIES
3 c. milk
4 eggs

¼ c. honey
½ tsp. vanilla extract
¼ tsp. ground nutmeg

Beat together milk, eggs, honey, vanilla and nutmeg using a blender, food processor or electric mixer. Pour the mixture into six individual cups or one 6-cup baking dish. Put in the strawberries, dividing them equally if you use individual cups. Put the cups or baking dish into a pan of hot water and bake in a preheated oven 350° 20-40 minutes depending on the size of the cups. Remove the custard from the oven before it is fully set and allow it to cool standing in the pan of hot water. This will finish cooking the custard without its becoming "weepy" although liquid sometimes accumulates around the strawberry which float on top of the custard. Yield: 6 servings.

STRAWBERRY-ORANGE YOGURT DESSERT

FSGA Women's Committee

4 c. whole fresh Florida
 STRAWBERRIES
½ c. orange juice

⅔ c. brown sugar
2 c. plain yogurt

(continued)

Wash and hull Florida strawberries and drain them on a towel. Marinate them in the orange juice for 1 hour. Combine the brown sugar and yogurt. Stir in the strawberries and the juice in which they were marinating. Serve in tall stemmed glasses. Yield: 6-8.

STRAWBERRY ICE CREAM

FSGA Women's Committee

2 c. sliced Florida
  STRAWBERRIES
½ c. sugar
2 c. heavy cream

2 c. light cream
½ c. sugar
1 tsp. vanilla extract
⅛ tsp. salt

Combine the sliced Florida strawberries and sugar and refrigerate for 24 hours. The juice from the berries will combine with the sugar to form a syrup. To make the ice cream purée the strawberries and sugar. Combine the purée with the heavy and light cream, sugar, vanilla, and salt in the processing canister of your ice cream churn. Stir until the sugar dissolves, then pack the churn with salt and ice, and churn and harden the ice cream according to directions for your unit. Yield: 6 cups.

STRAWBERRY SHERBET

FSGA Women's Committee

1½ c. unsweetened Florida
  STRAWBERRY purée
2 c. water
¾ c. sugar

1 env. unflavored gelatin
¼ c. lemon juice
2 egg whites

Mix the sugar and water in a saucepan bring to a boil and cook at a full boil for about 5 minutes or until the mixture becomes syrupy. Soften the gelatin in the lemon juice and stir it into the hot syrup. Stir in the strawberry purée. Chill. To make sherbet beat the egg whites until they are glossy and hold firm peaks. Fold into the strawberry mixture. Pour the sherbet unto the processing canister of your ice cream churn, pack with salt and ice, then churn and harden according to the directions for your unit. Yield: 6 cups.

MOLDED STRAWBERRY CREAM

FSGA Women's Committee

2 c. unsweetened Florida
  STRAWBERRY purée
1 env. unflavored gelatin
¼ c. cold water
1 c. sugar

2 c. whipping cream
½ tsp. vanilla extract
Fresh mint leaves and orange
  slices for garnish

Soften the gelatin in the water, then heat until it dissolves. Combine it with the strawberry purée and sugar. Stir until sugar dissolves. Chill

(continued)

34491B-00

about 20 minutes. Whip the cream until it forms soft peaks; whip in vanilla. Fold the whipped cream into the strawberry purée and pour into an oiled 6-cup mold. Chill at least 3 hours before serving. To serve, unmold onto a chilled platter and garnish with mint leaves and thin slices of orange. Yield: 12 servings.

OLD FASHIONED STRAWBERRY ICE CREAM

FSGA Women's Committee

6½ c. Florida STRAWBERRIES
1½ T. lemon juice
1 c. sugar

½ c. water
3 egg yolks
2 c. light cream

Purée the strawberries with the lemon juice and refrigerate. Combine the sugar and water in a saucepan and bring to a boil. Cook and stir until the sugar dissolves and the syrup reaches 230° on a candy thermometer. Beat the egg yolks until light and foamy with the mixer on high, gradually pour the hot sugar syrup into the egg yolks, beating constantly until the mixture is cooled and thickened. Stir in the cream and strawberry purée. If you want the ice cream to be sweeter add honey to taste. Chill the mixture until you are ready to process. Pour the ice cream base into the processing canister of your ice cream churn. Pack with ice and salt, then churn and harden according to directions for your unit. Yield: about 6 cups.

STRAWBERRY CHEESECAKE ICE CREAM

FSGA Women's Committee

3 pt. chopped STRAWBERRIES
16 oz. cream cheese, softened
3 eggs
1 (14-oz.) can sweetened
  condensed milk

1 (12-oz.) can evaporated milk
10 c. milk
2 c. sugar

Beat cream cheese and sugar in mixer bowl until smooth. Add eggs, mix well. Stir in condensed milk, evaporated milk, strawberries and 8 cups milk. Pour into 5-quart ice cream freezer container. Add 2 cups milk or enough milk to fill to fill line. Freeze using manufacturer's instructions.

STRAWBERRY MOUSSE

FSGA Women's Committee

2 pt. fresh STRAWBERRIES
2 env. gelatin
¾ c. sugar
½ c. cold water

1 T. lemon juice
2 T. Kirsch of Framboise liqueur
3 egg whites
1 c. heavy cream

Purée strawberries in blender. Mix gelatin and ½ cup of the sugar; stir in water; cook over low heat until dissolved. Stir into purée; add lemon

(continued)

and Kirsch. Refrigerate about 30 minutes while you beat the egg whites until stiff and add the rest of the sugar. Beat cream. Fold into purée and chill.

FRESH STRAWBERRY FROST

FSGA Women's Committee

3 pt. fresh STRAWBERRIES
2 c. sugar
1½ c. orange juice
½ c. lemon juice
¼ c. Grand Mariner

Place half the strawberries, half the sugar, half the orange juice and half the lemon juice in electric blender container. Cover; turn motor to high speed and blend for 30 seconds. Pour mixture in 12 x 8 x 2-inch baking dish. Repeat, using remaining strawberries, sugar and juices. Stir in Grand Mariner; freeze until partially frozen. Turn into bowl; beat with electric mixer at medium speed until smooth. Return mixture to baking dish and freeze until firm. Cover with foil and store in freezer for several days. Flavor mellows with refreezing. Remove from freezer for 10 minutes or until just soft enough to spoon into sherbet glasses. Serve at once.

STRAWBERRY ICE CREAM

FSGA Women's Committee

1 pt. chopped fresh
  STRAWBERRIES
⅔ c. evaporated milk
¼ c. sugar
Dash of salt

Place milk in ice tray; chill until ice crystals begin to form around edges. Mix strawberries, sugar, salt; let stand. Place ice cold milk into cold quart bowl; whip with cold beater until fluffy. Fold in strawberry mixture; freeze until solid.

STRAWBERRY CROWN

FSGA Women's Committee

2 pt. chopped fresh
  STRAWBERRIES
1 c. sugar
8 lady fingers, split
1 qt. vanilla ice cream

Cook chopped strawberries and sugar in medium saucepan. Heat to boiling; cook stirring often, 15 minutes. Cool completely. Butter a 6-inch springform pan; stand lady fingers ¼ inch apart around edge. Arrange remaining lady fingers on bottom. Spoon ⅓ of the ice cream into pan; drizzle with ¼ cups strawberry sauce. Make 2 more layers of ice cream and sauce; reserving any remaining sauce; freeze. Loosen dessert around edge with knife to serve; remove side of pan. Place dessert on

(continued)

34491B-00

metal base on a serving plate. Garnish with additional whole strawberries; drizzle with reserved remaining sauce.

Recipe Favorites

Recipe Favorites

34491B-00

Interesting and Unique

Berries in Parfait Glass

Everything from dips and sauces to strawberry pancakes and everything in between

INTERESTING & UNIQUE

STRAWBERRY POPS

Erin Freel Best

8-12 lg. STRAWBERRIES
3-oz. pkg. cream cheese,
  softened

2 T. powdered sugar
1 T. sour cream

Remove stems from berries, forming a flat base. Place berries pointed end up. With sharp knife, carefully slice berries in half vertically through center to within 1/4 inch of base. Cut each half into 3 wedges, forming 6 petals. (Do not slice through base.) Pull petals apart slightly. In a small bowl, beat cream cheese, sugar and sour cream until light and fluffy. Fill berries with mixture.

FRUTTA CARAMELLATA

FSGA Women's Committee

12 sm. STRAWBERRIES
Vegetable oil for brushing foil
1 mandarin orange, such as
  clementine

About 24 wooden skewers
2 c. sugar

Lightly brush a large sheet of foil with oil. Remove leaves from strawberries, leaving base and stems attached. Peel orange and separate into sections, discarding pith and membranes. Pat all fruit dry. Hold 1 strawberry, stem end down and carefully insert a skewer into side of strawberry until secure (do not push skewer all the way through strawberry). Skewer remaining strawberries in same manner. Skewer 1 orange section crosswise through thickest part (do not push skewer all the way through section). Skewer remaining sections in same manner. In a dry 3-quart heavy saucepan cook sugar over moderately low heat, stirring slowly with a fork (to help sugar melt evenly) until melted and pale golden. Cook caramel, without stirring, swirling pan (to ensure even coloring) until deep golden. Remove pan from heat. Work very quickly and carefully and tilting saucepan, dip 1 piece of fruit into caramel, turning fruit to coat evenly. Arrange fruit on foil and immediately twist skewer, removing it. Repeat procedure with remaining fruit in same manner, arranging in one layer on foil. Let caramelized fruit stand until coating is hardened, about 2 minutes. Carefully peel fruit from foil and transfer to a metal rack set in shallow baking pan (fruit juices may drip) arranging one layer. Cool fruit slightly, about 15 minutes. Fruit may be caramelized 1 1/2 hours ahead. Serves 6.

CHUNKY STRAWBERRY APPLESAUCE

FSGA Women's Committee

1 (1-pt.) basket fresh
STRAWBERRIES, hulled,
halved
2½ lbs. sm. Red Delicious
apples, about 6 med.
quartered, cored, cut into

1-inch pieces
2 c. hot water
1 (3-oz.) pkg. strawberry
flavored gelatin
2 tsp. fresh lemon juice, opt.

Cook apples, water and strawberries in covered heavy medium saucepan over medium-low heat until apples are falling apart tender, stirring occasionally, about 40 minutes. Mix in gelatin and stir until dissolved. Adjust tartness with lemon juice, if desired. Cover and let cool. Refrigerate until cold and thickened, at least 2 hours. Serves 4-6.

STRAWBERRY SALSA

FSGA Women's Committee

1 c. finely chopped
STRAWBERRIES
1 fresh serrano or jalapeño chili
¼ c. finely chopped white onion
2 T. finely chopped fresh
coriander

½ tsp. fresh lime juice
¼ tsp. salt
½ tsp. sugar if desired

Wearing rubber gloves, remove stems, seed and ribs from chili and chop fine. In a bowl stir together chili and remaining salsa ingredients.

STRAWBERRY SAUTÉ

FSGA Women's Committee

2 c. halved or quartered fresh
STRAWBERRIES
3 T. butter
¼ c. coarsely chopped walnuts

3 T. dark brown sugar
3 T. grated semi-sweet
chocolate
¼ c. crumbled cookies

In medium skillet, melt butter until bubbly. Add walnuts; cook and stir briefly, just until nuts begin to color. Add brown sugar and stir for less than 30 seconds. Remove pan from heat. Add strawberries and chocolate. Quickly stir to coat berries and melt chocolate. Spoon over ice cream custard pie or angel food cake. Sprinkle with crumbled cookies. Serves 4.

34491B-00

CHOCOLATE-DIPPED STRAWBERRIES

FSGA Women's Committee

4-6 c. fresh STRAWBERRIES,
 washed
8-oz. Ghirardelli broken milk
 chocolate or any bittersweet,
 white or sweet dark milk or
 semi sweet chocolate

Cut fruit into bite-size chunks. Make sure fruit is dry. Chop chocolate into very small pieces. Melt chocolate in top of double boiler over simmering, not boiling, water, stirring constantly until smooth. Remove from heat and tilt pans so that all chocolate comes to the side. Using a toothpick pierce fruit chunk and dip into chocolate about ¼ inch from the top, then turn up side down to catch the drips. Place dipped fruit in fluted foil cupcake liners with aluminum foil. Firm in freezer 10 minutes or refrigerate ½ hour. Serve same day.

STRAWBERRY NUT ROLL

FSGA Women's Committee

1 c. sliced fresh
 STRAWBERRIES, lightly
 sugared
6 eggs, separated

¾ c. sugar
1 tsp. baking powder
1½ c. grated pecans
2 c. heavy cream

Grease jelly roll pan, line with waxed paper; grease paper. Beat the egg yolks with the sugar until thick. Mix baking powder and pecans and fold into yolks. Whip the egg whites stiff; fold into batter; spread in pan, bake at 350° for 20 minutes. Cover with damp towel, chill in refrigerator. Turn cake out on towel, remove paper. Whip 1½ cup cream until stiff and add strawberries. Spread on cake. Roll like a jelly roll and chill until serving time. Whip the additional cream and serve with nut roll. Garnish.

STRAWBERRY FONDUE FRITTERS

FSGA Women's Committee

1 pt. fresh whole
 STRAWBERRIES, stemmed
1 c. buttermilk baking mix
½ c. water

1 egg
¼ tsp. almond extract
Salad oil
Confectioners' sugar

Beat baking mix, water, egg and extract with rotary mixer until smooth. Pour oil into metal fondue pat to depth of 1 to 1½ inches. Heat on fondue stand over burner or on range to 375° or until 1-inch bread cube browns in 1 minute. With long handled fork, each person dips strawberry into batter, cooks it in hot oil until puffed and golden brown, then rolls fritter in confectioners' sugar.

STRAWBERRIES AND BANANAS WITH SABAYON SAUCE

FSGA Women's Committee

1 pt. fresh STRAWBERRIES,
  sliced
2 egg yolks
2 T. sugar

2 T. sweet Marsala wine
3 T. orange juice
3 bananas, sliced

Combine egg yolks and sugar in the top of a double boiler over simmering water. Whisking constantly, add wine and cook about 5 minutes or until mixture thickens. Transfer to a small bowl; cover and chill 30 minutes. In a medium bowl, sprinkle orange juice over banana slices. Add strawberries and toss lightly. To serve, spoon fruit mixture into serving dish and top with chilled sauce.

TRIPLE BERRY WAKE-UP BREAKFAST

Sue Harrell

1/2 pt. fresh STRAWBERRIES,
  sliced
1/4 c. fat free cream cheese,
  softened
2 T. strawberry spreadable fruit
4 slices white bread, crusts
  removed

1 egg
2 T. skim milk
Strawberry syrup or
  confectioners' sugar, opt.

Combine cream cheese and spreadable fruit; spread on 2 slices of bread. Top with sliced berries, making a complete blanket over the cheese. Top each with the remaining bread. In a bowl, beat egg and milk. Heat a frying pan or griddle coated with non stick cooking spray over medium heat. Dip sandwiches in egg mixture and fry until golden brown on both sides. If desired, serve with syrup or dust with confectioners' sugar.

STRAWBERRIES WITH LEMON CREAM

FSGA Women's Committee

1 pt. fresh sliced
  STRAWBERRIES
1 T. sugar

1 c. light whipped topping
2 ctn. non fat lemon yogurt
1 T. grated lemon peel

Place strawberries in a medium bowl; sprinkle with sugar. In another bowl, fold whipped topping into yogurt; add lemon peel. To serve, layer strawberries and yogurt mixture in 4 parfait glasses.

34491B-00

LOW FAT DESSERT NACHOS WITH FRUIT SALSA

FSGA Women's Committee

2 c. chopped STRAWBERRIES
2 kiwi fruit, peeled, chopped
1 (11-oz.) can mandarin
  oranges, drained
10 flour tortillas

⅓ c. sugar
1 tsp. cinnamon
8 oz. Neufchatel cheese
3 T. honey
½ c. orange juice

Combine strawberries, kiwi fruit and mandarin oranges in bowl, mix well. Chill, covered in refrigerator. Brush on side of tortillas lightly with water. Cut each tortilla into 6 wedges. Dip one side of each wedge in mixture of sugar and cinnamon. Place on greased foil lined baking sheet. Bake at 500° for 4 minutes or until brown and crisp. Remove to wire rack to cool. Combine cheese, honey and orange juice in saucepan. Whisk over low heat until smooth. Mound chips on platter. Serve with fruit salsa and cheese sauce.

FROZEN STRAWBERRY CRUNCH

FSGA Women's Committee

1 pt. fresh chopped
  STRAWBERRIES
2 pkgs. strawberry Jello
1 c. hot water

1 c. chopped nuts
1 lg. can crushed pineapple
1 ctn. sour cream

Mix Jello and hot water; combine with strawberries, nuts and pineapple. Pour ½ of the ingredients into oblong Pyrex dish. Place in freezer for 40 minutes. Pour sour cream over Jello; place back in freezer until firm. Spoon on remaining Jello carefully; freeze again. Cut and serve.

STRAWBERRY WITH CANNOLI CREAM

FSGA Women's Committee

2 qt. fresh STRAWBERRIES,
  quartered
½ c. part skim ricotta
2 T. confectioners' sugar
⅛ tsp. grated orange peel

2 T. orange juice
½ tsp. vanilla extract
2 drops almond extract
2 tsp. chopped semi-sweet
  chocolate

In food processor or blender, combine ricotta, sugar, orange peel and juice, vanilla and almond extracts. Process or blend until very smooth. Stir in chocolate. Cover and refrigerate until ready to serve. To serve, divide berries among bowls or stemmed glasses. Stir cream and pour over berries.

MEXICAN CHOCOLATE SAUCE OVER STRAWBERRIES

FSGA Women's Committee

2 qt. fresh STRAWBERRIES,
  quartered
3-oz. semi-sweet chocolate
  chopped, or morsels
3 T. Kahlua
2 T. milk

1 T. light brown sugar
2 tsp. vanilla extract
$1/4$ tsp. ground cinnamon
Unsweetened whipped cream
$1^1/2$ T. toasted slivered almonds

In a small saucepan over low heat, stir chocolate, Kahlua, milk, brown sugar, vanilla and cinnamon until smooth and shiny. Divide berries among four serving dishes or stemmed glasses. Spoon sauce over to serve. Top with whipped cream and almonds.

STRAWBERRIES WITH CHOCOLATE-COCONUT FUDGE

FSGA Women's Committee

2 qt. fresh STRAWBERRIES,
  quartered
3-oz. milk chocolate, chopped or
  morsels

5 T. canned coconut milk
3 T. toasted shredded coconut

In a small saucepan cover low heat, stir chocolate and coconut milk until smooth and lustrous. Divide the berries among serving dishes or stemmed glasses and spoon warm sauce over. Sprinkle with shredded coconut to serve.

Note: Sauce can be made ahead and refrigerated. Reheat over low heat or in microwave at 50% power.

STRAWBERRY MERINGUES GLACE

FSGA Women's Committee

1 tsp. chopped fresh
  STRAWBERRIES
$1/8$ tsp. salt
$1/2$ tsp. cream of tartar

2 egg whites
$1/2$ c. sugar
$1/2$ tsp. vanilla extract
1 pt. strawberry ice cream

Preheat oven to 250°. Combine salt, cream of tartar and egg whites; beat with rotary beater until foamy. Gradually add sugar; continue beating until stiff. Add vanilla. Spoon some meringue onto lightly buttered brown paper placed on cookie sheet; flatten into 4 thin bases about $1^1/2$ inches in diameter. Surround bases with remaining meringue to height of 2 inches, leaving centers unfilled. Bake for 1 hour 15 minutes. Transfer paper to damp board; remove meringues with spatula. Fill with ice cream and top with strawberries when meringues are cold. Yield: 4 servings.

34491B-00

ANGEL HAIR PASTA WITH STRAWBERRY AND BROWN SUGAR SAUCE

FSGA Women's Committee

1 c. thinly sliced fresh
STRAWBERRIES
⅓ c. dark brown sugar

¾ c. heavy cream
4-oz. angel hair pasta
2 T. chopped, toasted hazelnuts

In small bowl, toss strawberries and 1 tablespoon brown sugar. Cover and set aside. In medium saucepan, combine cream and remaining brown sugar. Bring to boil, stirring constantly. Reduce heat and simmer several minutes or until sugar is dissolved and cream is light brown in color and smooth in consistency. Remove from heat. Meanwhile, cook pasta according to package directions omitting salt. Drain very well. Return to saucepan to heat, add pasta and toss until thoroughly coated and heated. Place pasta in serving bowl or individual dishes. Spoon strawberries and juices over pasta. Sprinkle chopped nuts. Serve immediately. Serves 4.

STRAWBERRY DIP

Rose Peacock

1 c. chilled fresh cream
1 (6-oz.) can frozen pineapple
concentrate, thawed
1 T. fresh lemon juice

2 T. powdered sugar
2-3 T. grated ginger root
1 (8-oz.) cream cheese

Whip cream until fluffy. Beat in pineapple and lemon juice gradually. Stir in sugar and ginger. Refrigerate to blend flavors for 2 hours. Beat cream to fluff and fold in cream cheese. Find large sweet Florida strawberries with stems and start dipping!

VALENTINE BERRIES & CREAM

Selma Gale

1½ c. Florida STRAWBERRIES,
halved
8 squares (1-oz.) semi-sweet
chocolate
1 T. shortening
2 (3-oz.) pkgs. cream cheese

¼ c. butter
1½ c. confectioners' sugar
⅓ c. cocoa
2 T. milk
1 tsp. vanilla extract
2½ c. whipping cream

Line a 9-inch heart shaped baking pan with foil; set aside. In a heavy saucepan over low heat, melt chocolate and shortening; stir until smooth. Pour into prepared pan, swirling to coat the bottom and 1½-inch up the sides. Refrigerate for 1 minute, then swirl the chocolate to reinforce the heart. Refrigerate for 30 minutes or until firm. Using foil, lift from pan, remove foil and place heart on a serving plate. In a mixing bowl, beat the cream cheese and butter until smooth. Combine confec-

(continued)

tioners' sugar and cocoa add to creamed mixture with milk and vanilla. Beat until smooth. Gently fold ²/₃ of the whipped cream into cream cheese mixture. Spoon into heart. Insert star tip #32 into a pastry bag, fill with remaining whipped cream. Pipe around edge of heart. Garnish with fresh Florida strawberries, sliced or whole. Yield: 8-10 servings.

STRAWBERRY SOUR CREAM OMELET

FSGA Women's Committee

1 pt. fresh Florida
  STRAWBERRIES, sliced
5 eggs, separated
8 oz. sour cream

½ tsp. salt
2 T. butter
Powdered sugar, opt.

Beat egg yolks until thick and lemon colored. Add ½ cup sour cream and salt. Beat until blended. Beat egg whites, (at room temperature) until soft peaks form; fold into yolk mixture. Heat a 10-inch skillet over medium heat. Add butter and rotate to coat bottom of pan. Pour egg mixture into skillet. Cook over low heat 8-10 minutes. Remove from heat and bake at 350° for 12-15 minutes or until golden brown. Loosen omelet with a spatula, fold in half, gently slide onto serving plate. Top with remaining sour cream and strawberries. Dust with powdered sugar. Yield: 6 servings.

STRAWBERRY WHIP

FSGA Women's Committee

1½ c. sliced BERRIES
1 heaping cup of powdered
  sugar

1 egg white

With an electric mixer beat until smooth berries, powdered sugar and egg white. Whip until it peaks. Serve on angel food cake, pound cake or tea loaf.

FLORIDA STRAWBERRY WINE SAUCE

FSGA Women's Committee

2 c. fresh Florida
  STRAWBERRIES, mashed
¼ c. water

½ c. red wine
¼ c. sugar

Combine 1 cup berries, water, wine and sugar. Cook in saucepan until thickened. (can be done in microwave). Strain mixture, pressing solids through strainer. Stir in remaining berries. Refrigerate for 3 hours. Serve over pound cake, ice cream or fruit salads.

34491B-00

STRAWBERRIES AND KAHLUA DIP

FSGA Women's Committee

2 qt. fresh Florida
  STRAWBERRIES
1 (8 oz.) cream cheese

2 T. brown sugar
1 c. marshmallow creme
1 T. Kahlua, or more to taste

Combine cream cheese, brown sugar, marshmallow creme and Kahlua. Mix well and chill. Serve with fresh strawberries.

STRAWBERRIES & PINA COLADA DIP

FSGA Women's Committee

2 c. pineapple yogurt, not Swiss
  style
1 (8-oz.) ctn. frozen whipped
  topping, thawed

2 pkg. pina colada mix
Flaked coconut to taste

Mix together yogurt, whipped topping and pina colada mix. Refrigerate overnight. Serve in a hollowed out cantaloupe or pineapple surrounded by strawberries. Garnish with fresh mint.

STRAWBERRY ROMANOFF

FSGA Women's Committee

4 c. whole Florida
  STRAWBERRIES, hulled
1/4 c. sugar
1/4 c. Grand Mariner
1 c. whipping cream

2 T. sugar
2 T. Grand Mariner
1/8 tsp. cinnamon
1/3 c. sour cream
3 T. toasted almonds

Combine 1/4 cup sugar and 1/4 cup Grand Mariner in a large bowl; stir until sugar dissolves. Add strawberries, toss gently and set aside. Beat whipping cream until foamy; gradually add 2 tablespoons sugar and 2 tablespoons Grand Mariner and cinnamon beating until soft peaks form. Fold in sour cream. Spoon strawberries and syrup into small serving dishes. Top each with a dollop of cream mixture; sprinkle with nuts.

STRAWBERRIES MARSALA

FSGA Women's Committee

8 c. fresh Florida
  STRAWBERRIES, capped
2 T. plus 2 tsp. Marsala wine

1 T. plus 1 tsp. sugar
1/2 tsp. lemon juice

Combine wine, sugar and lemon juice in a large bowl. Add Florida strawberries and toss gently. Cover and chill 8 hours. Toss before serving.

STRAWBERRY COCONUT NESTS

FSGA Women's Committee

1½ c. fresh Florida
  STRAWBERRIES, sliced
1 T. sugar
8 oz. cream cheese, softened
½ c. sugar

2 tsp. milk
1 tsp. vanilla extract
6 commercial shortcake cups
½ c. toasted flaked coconut

Combine Florida strawberries and 1 tablespoon sugar, stir gently. Set aside. Combine cream cheese, ½ cup sugar, milk and vanilla, beat at medium speed of electric mixer until smooth. Spread over top and sides of shortcake cups, sprinkle with coconut. Place on individual serving plates. Spoon ¼ cup strawberries into each. Serve immediately.

STRAWBERRIES IN A CLOUD

FSGA Women's Committee

¾ c. halved Florida
  STRAWBERRIES
½ c. whipping cream
¼ c. powdered sugar
½ c. sour cream

1 tsp. grated lemon peel
6 single serve graham cracker
  crust
¾ c. blueberries

In a small bowl combine whipping cream and powdered sugar; beat at low speed until well mixed scraping side of bowl occasionally. Beat at high speed until peaks form. Fold in sour cream and lemon peel. Gently fold in strawberries and blueberries. Spoon mixture evenly into crusts. Refrigerate 1 hour before serving. If desired garnish with whole strawberries (fanned). Store in refrigerator. Yield: 6 tarts.

Note: A nine inch graham cracker crust can be substituted.

STRAWBERRY CHOCOLATE

FSGA Women's Committee

2 pt. Florida STRAWBERRIES
2 pt. heavy cream
2 boxes chocolate wafer
  cookies

⅓ c. sweet sherry
1½ c. caramel sauce

Wash, dry, hull and thinly slice strawberries, reserving 6 whole strawberries for garnish; set aside. In a medium mixing bowl whip cream until it forms stiff peaks; set aside. In a 9-inch square pan or a decorative serving bowl, place a single layer of chocolate wafers. Brush wafers with sherry. Spread ½ cup of caramel sauce over wafers. Next layer ⅓ of the berries in the dish and then ⅓ of the whipped cream. Repeat complete layering process twice. Garnish with whole strawberries and any remaining chocolate wafer crumbs. Chill 4-6 hours before serving. Yield: 6-8 servings.

34491B-00

MARINATED STRAWBERRIES IN RUM

FSGA Women's Committee

1 pt. Florida STRAWBERRIES
¼ c. light rum
⅓ c. sour cream

¼ c. confectioners' sugar
1 T. toasted coconut

Hull strawberries and slice. Combine in a small bowl, the strawberries and rum. Set aside for at least 15 minutes. Combine in another small bowl sour cream and sugar. To serve spoon strawberries into 4 stemmed glasses. Top with sour cream mixture. Garnish with toasted coconut. To toast coconut, place on a baking pan and bake in a preheated 350° oven until golden brown about 5 minutes. Makes 4 servings.

STRAWBERRY MARSHMALLOW WHIP

FSGA Women's Committee

1½ c. crushed Florida
  STRAWBERRIES
14 graham crackers
¼ c. melted butter
1 c. milk

½ lb. (32) marshmallows, cut
1 T. lemon juice
¼ tsp. salt
1 c. heavy cream

Crumble graham crackers add melted butter. Mix well. Press cracker crust into a greased 8 x 8-inch pan. Combine milk and marshmallows. Heat stirring occasionally until marshmallows are melted. Set aside until cold. Combine strawberries, lemon juice, salt, and heavy cream. Add to marshmallow mixture. Pour into crust. Chill overnight before serving. Makes 6 servings.

MARINATED STRAWBERRIES

FSGA Women's Committee

1 qt. Florida STRAWBERRIES,
  halved
⅔ c. brown sugar

⅜ c. orange juice
1 pt. sour cream

Marinate the strawberries in the orange juice for 1 hour. Mix sugar and sour cream and blend with strawberries. Top with one whole berry when serving.

BOWL WITH BERRIES

FSGA Women's Committee

1½ c. Florida STRAWBERRIES
1 lg. banana
4-5 medium size peaches
2 rounded T. sugar

2 lg. bottles champagne
5 apricots
¼ c. brandy

(continued)

Slice peaches, bananas, apricots, and strawberries into a large bowl. Add sugar, brandy, and 1½ cups champagne, or just enough to not quite cover the fruit. Stir. Marinade in refrigerator about 2 hours, stirring several times. Just before serving add rest of chilled champagne. Mix well, strain; pour into well chilled glasses. Serve immediately.

STRAWBERRIES IN BASKETS

FSGA Women's Committee

Baskets:

1 box filo dough

2 sticks of unsalted butter, melted

10 T. of ground dry bread crumbs

Strawberry filling:

½ c. chopped Florida STRAWBERRIES

2 qt. Florida STRAWBERRIES, cleaned and capped

24 (2-oz.) cream cheese, room temperature

1 c. powdered sugar

Chocolate Sauce:

⅔ c. light Karo syrup

½ c. whipping cream

8 oz. Baker's semi-sweet chocolate

2 T. paraffin shavings

Baskets: Preheat oven to 350°. Place out one sheet of filo on cutting board, brush with melted butter and sprinkle with one tablespoon bread crumbs. Repeat this procedure three more times with each additional layer of dough placed on the previous layer. Top with fifth sheet and brush with butter. Keep unused filo covered with damp cloth. Cut into 2-inch squares and put into miniature muffin pans. Repeat this entire procedure. Bake at 350° for 10-12 minutes. Store in airtight container at room temperature. Baskets will remain fresh for up to 2 weeks if stored in air tight container. Makes approximately 84 baskets. **Strawberry filling:** Mix the chopped strawberries, cream cheese and powdered sugar in food processor. Place in refrigerator. This may be made 24 hours ahead. Fill each basket ¾ full, one hour before serving time. Add a whole strawberry, drizzled in chocolate to each basket. Serve at room temperature. **Chocolate Sauce:** In medium saucepan stir corn syrup and cream. Bring to a boil over medium heat. Remove from heat. Add chocolate and paraffin and stir until completely melted. Let completely cool, then drizzle over strawberry tips. Place tip pointed up in the center of each filled baskets. Yield: 40 servings.

34491B-00

STRAWBERRY DRESSING

FSGA Women's Committee

1 c. Florida STRAWBERRIES
½ c. sugar
½ c. currant jelly

⅓ c. water
4 T. cornstarch
2 T. lemon juice

Combine berries, sugar, jelly and water; bring to a boil and simmer for 15 minutes. Mix cornstarch with 2 tablespoons water and stir into hot mixture. Cook one more minute through a sieve. Chill. Serve dressing over mixed fruits such as peaches, pears, bananas, grapes, apples and oranges.

ALMOND CREAM STRAWBERRIES

FSGA Women's Committee

2 pt. fresh Florida
  STRAWBERRIES
1 (3-oz.) pkg. vanilla instant
  pudding

1 c. milk
1 tsp. almond extract
½ pt. whipped cream, whipped

Cut stem ends off strawberries. Cut deep "X" in top of each berry. Gently spread apart to form "Petals", set aside. Prepare instant pudding using only 1 cup milk; gently fold in whipped cream and almond extract into pudding. Spoon cream mixture into decorating bag with longer tip. Pipe cream into strawberries. Refrigerate until ready to serve.

FRESH STRAWBERRY BANANA OMELETS

Teresa Griffin

1 c. fresh STRAWBERRIES,
  hulled and sliced
1 banana, peeled and sliced
1½ T. sugar
2 T. butter divided

¼ tsp. grated lemon peel
1 T. fresh lemon juice
¼ tsp. salt
¼ c. water

Combine strawberries, bananas, sugar, lemon peel and juice in medium bowl, mix lightly. Cover; let stand 15 minutes. Meanwhile, mix eggs, salt and water with fork in small bowl. Heat 1 tablespoon butter in 8-inch omelet pan or skillet over medium-high heat until just hot enough to sizzle a drop of water. Pour in half of egg mixture (approximately ½ cup). Mixture should set at edges at once. With back of pancake turner, carefully push cooked portions of edges toward center so that uncooked portions flow to bottom. Slide pan rapidly back and forth over heat to keep mixture in motion and sliding freely. While top is still moist and creamy looking, spoon ½ cup fruit mixture over half of omelet. With pancake turner, fold in half, turn onto heated platter. Keep warm. Repeat with remaining egg mixture and ½ cup fruit mixture. Top omelets with remaining fruit.

STRAWBERRY SYRUP

Dee Dee Grooms

4 c. ripe STRAWBERRIES,
  rinsed and hulled
1³/₄ c. water

2 tsp. finely grated lemon zest
1¹/₄ c. granulated sugar

Crush the berries in a heavy saucepan. Add 1 cup water and the lemon zest. Bring to a boil, reduce the heat slightly and simmer over medium heat for 5 minutes, skimming any foam off the top. Set the mixture aside to cool. Meanwhile, place the sugar and the remaining ³/₄ cup water in a small, heavy saucepan. Bring to a boil and cook until the syrup reaches 260° on a candy thermometer. Set aside. Strain cooled strawberry mixture through a double thickness of cheesecloth. Squeeze well until all the juice and pulp are extracted and the seeds are left behind. Discard the cheese cloth contents. Pour the clear, strained liquid into a heavy saucepan with the sugar syrup. Bring to a boil and cook for 8 minutes. Pack in 2 sterilized half pint jars, leaving ¹/₄-inch of head space. Process in a boiling water bath for 10 minutes.

STRAWBERRY FONDUE

Dee Dee Grooms

Fritter Batter:

STRAWBERRIES, whole,
  washed, dried and stemmed
1 c. sifted flour
3 T. sugar
1¹/₂ tsp. baking powder
¹/₂ tsp. salt

2 eggs, beaten
¹/₃ c. milk
1 T. melted butter
Cooking oil
Powdered sugar

Fill metal fondue pot half full with cooking oil. Heat to 350°. Place pot on fondue stand over flame and maintain temperature. Spear each strawberry, (whole, washed, dried and stemmed). Next, dip the strawberry into the batter. Then plunge into the hot cooking oil. Dip into powdered sugar. Makes enough batter for about 1 pint of strawberries.

CHOCOLATE COVERED STRAWBERRIES

Dee Dee Grooms

1 qt. STRAWBERRIES
3 T. margarine
3 T. light corn syrup
¹/₄ tsp. salt

2 c. powdered sugar
1 (12-oz.) pkg. chocolate chips
  (semi-sweet)
¹/₂ stick paraffin

Combine margarine, corn syrup, salt and powdered sugar and pat around berries. Let berries sit for 2 hours in the refrigerator before dipping in chocolate. Place on wax paper lined cookie sheet. Then melt

(continued)

34491B-00

chocolate and paraffin wax in double boiler. Dip each berry and place on wax paper.

ALMOND CREAM STRAWBERRIES

Teresa Griffin

2 pt. lg. STRAWBERRIES
1 (3⅜ to 3¾-oz.) pkg. vanilla
  instant pudding
1 c. milk

1 c. heavy or whipping cream,
  whipped
1 tsp. almond extract

Cut stem ends off strawberries. Cut a deep "X" in tip of each berry and gently spread apart to make "petals"; set aside. Prepare instant pudding as label direct but use only 1 cup milk. With wire whisk or rubber spatula, gently fold whipped cream and almond extract into prepared instant pudding. Spoon cream mixture into decorating bag with large writing tube. Pipe cream into strawberries. Serve immediately, or refrigerate until serving.

STRAWBERRIES REBECCA

Teresa Griffin

2 qt. fresh STRAWBERRIES,
  washed, and stemmed
2 c. sour cream
1 c. light brown sugar

1 T. vanilla
1 T. cinnamon
Fresh mint for garnish

Place berries in large bowl or small dessert dishes. Combine sour cream, light brown sugar, vanilla, and cinnamon. Spoon over berries, garnish with mint. Sauce can be made ahead and refrigerated. Serves 8.

STRAWBERRY BLOSSOMS

Teresa Griffin

1 (10-oz.) pkg. frozen
  STRAWBERRIES in syrup,
  partially thawed
1 (6-oz.) can frozen pink
  lemonade concentrate, thawed

1 pt. vanilla ice cream
1 c. milk
Fresh STRAWBERRIES

Combine the undrained strawberries, lemonade concentrate, ice cream and milk in a blender container or food processor. Process until smooth. Pour into glasses. Garnish each serving with a fresh strawberry. Serve immediately. Makes 4 servings.

STRAWBERRIES WITH LEMON AND SUGAR

Dolores Poage

1 qt. STRAWBERRIES
1 tsp. grated lemon zest

¼ c. fresh lemon juice
2 T. sugar

In a medium bowl, combine lemon zest, lemon juice, and sugar. Halve or quarter strawberries. Toss well. Can stand for up to 2 hours.

STRAWBERRIES ALA FLAMBE

Margaret Rodwell

1 pt. STRAWBERRIES, sliced in
half
¼ c. sugar

2 T. butter
2 T. brandy

Melt butter in sauté pan, and sugar. Bring to boil, while moving pan add strawberries. Remove from heat, add brandy, place over heat until brandy pan ignites. Serve with toothpicks.

LA HACIENDA TRADITIONAL SOPAIPILLAS

Teresa Griffin

Fresh STRAWBERRIES, sliced
1 c. flour
2 tsp. baking powder
1 T. salt
1 T. vegetable shortening
⅓ c. water, hot

Additional flour if needed
Peanut oil, 5 inches deep in pan
and heated to hot
1½ c. powdered sugar
Honey

In bowl, using hands or pastry blender, combine well; flour, baking powder, salt, vegetable shortening and water; be sure shortening is evenly distributed. Add water; stir with fork until dough consistency; knead 2-3 times. (If dough is dry; add a little more water; if wet, add 1-2 tablespoons flour.) Put dough in plastic bag, let rise for an hour in warm place. On lightly floured surface, roll dough into a rectangle ¼-inch thick. (If dough does not roll easily, cover, let rest a few minutes more, roll again, etc.); fold dough in half; roll to ⅓-inch rectangle again. Cut dough into ¾-inch rectangles. Fry 1-2 at a time, spooning oil over top to promote puffing. Drain on paper towels; dust with sugar; serve warm topped with honey and strawberries.

34491B-00

STRAWBERRY MANGO CHILI RELISH

Teresa Griffin

2 c. fresh STRAWBERRIES,
  sliced
Juice of 1 large lime
3 ripe mangos, peeled and diced
8 ripe peaches peeled and
  diced, blanching helps to peel
  peaches
1/4 tsp. coriander
5 several or jalapeño pepper,
  stemmed and diced

1/4 tsp. ground allspice
1 bunch green onions and tops,
  finely chopped
1 T. fresh mint, chopped
2 cloves garlic, finely diced
2 T. fresh cilantro, chopped
1 T. fresh chives, chopped
Salt and pepper to taste
1 1/2-oz. tequila, opt.

Cover fruits with juice. In a separate bowl, mix well remaining ingredients; gently toss into fruit. Adjust salt and pepper to taste; add more lime juice and tequila if desired. Cover, refrigerate at least one hour before serving. Wonderful accompaniment to grilled meats.

HAM WITH STRAWBERRY DIJON SAUCE

Dee Dee Grooms

1 qt. STRAWBERRIES, cleaned
  and halved
1 oven bag, lg. size (14 x
  20-inch)
2 T. all-purpose flour
2 (6-oz.) cans pineapple juice

3/4 c. honey
1/2 c. Grey Poupon Dijon
  mustard
1 (5-7-lb.) boneless fully cooked
  ham
Whole cloves

Preheat oven to 325°. Shake flour in oven bag; place in 13 x 9 x 2-inch baking pan. Add pineapple juice, honey and mustard to oven bag. Squeeze oven bag to blend ingredients. Using a table knife, lightly score surface of ham in a diamond pattern; insert cloves at intersections. Place ham in oven bag. Close oven bag with nylon tie; cut 6 (1/2-inch) slits in top. Bake for 1 3/4-2 1/4 hours or until meat thermometer reads 140°. To serve, cut open oven bag and transfer ham to serving platter. Stir strawberries into sauce in oven bag; serve with ham.

STRAWBERRIES ITALIANO

Erin Freel Best

1 qt. fresh STRAWBERRIES
3 T. balsamic vinegar
4 T. sugar
1/3 c. pine nuts

Pinch of ground cloves
1 pt. low or non fat vanilla
  frozen yogurt

Wash berries, remove hulls, and slice. Place in bowl. Mix vinegar and 3 tablespoons of the sugar. Pour over strawberries. Let sit 30 minutes. In heavy small skillet, over medium-low heat, cook the pine nuts, remaining

(continued)

sugar and ground cloves. Stir constantly. Cook until the pine nuts are golden and the sugar has melted. Scoop yogurt into four bowls. Add strawberries. Garnish with pine nuts. Serves 4

STRAWBERRIES WITH TOFFEE SAUCE

Erin Freel Best

1 qt. fresh STRAWBERRIES
¾ c. sugar
½ c. heavy cream
¼ c. light corn syrup

2 T. butter
½ c. chopped Heath toffee bars
1 c. sour cream

In a saucepan, combine sugar, cream, corn syrup and butter. Bring to a boil and cook for 3 minutes, stirring occasionally to prevent boiling over. Remove from heat and add candy. Stir until most of candy is dissolved. Cool. To serve, place strawberries in bowl, top with a dollop of sour cream and drizzle with sauce. Serves 6.

STRAWBERRY CREAM SQUARES

Erin Freel Best

20-z. frozen STRAWBERRIES
2 (3-oz.) pkgs. strawberry
  gelatin
2 c. boiling water

1 (13½-oz.) can crushed
  pineapple
2 lg. ripe bananas, finely diced
1 c. sour cream

Dissolve gelatin in boiling water. Add frozen strawberries; stir until thawed. Add pineapple and bananas. Pour half into 8 x 8 x 2-inch pan. Chill firm. Spread evenly with sour cream. Pour remaining gelatin atop. Chill firm. Cut in 9-inch square. Top with sour cream dollops.

STRAWBERRY GLAZE BANANAS

Margaret Rodwell

1 (10-oz.) pkg. frozen sliced
  STRAWBERRIES, thawed
1 T. sugar
⅔ c. water, divided

2½ T. cornstarch
⅛ tsp. red food coloring
1 T. lemon juice
1½ lb. bananas

Combine strawberries, sugar and ⅓ cup water in saucepan. Heat till boiling. Stir in cornstarch that has been dissolved in ⅓ cup water. Cook and stir till mixture boils. Reduce heat and simmer 3 minutes stirring. Remove from heat and add food color and lemon juice. Peel and slice bananas. Add to sauce and gently stir to coat bananas. Serve at room temperature.

110

SIMMERING CHICKEN STRAWBERRY KABOBS

Reggie Gordon

24 whole STRAWBERRIES
1 c. lemon juice
1 (12-oz.) can pineapple chunks
  with juice
Salt and pepper to taste

2 tsp. ground cinnamon
3 skinless, boneless chicken
  breasts, cubed
1 c. butter, melted
2 T. brown sugar

In a shallow glass bowl, combine lemon juice, juice from pineapple can, salt and pepper and 1 teaspoon cinnamon. Mix together. Add cubed chicken and marinate for 1 hour in the refrigerator. Preheat grill to medium heat. In a small bowl combine the melted butter or margarine, 1 teaspoon cinnamon, brown sugar and nutmeg. Lightly oil grate. Using metal or soaked wooden skewers arrange chicken, pineapple chunks and strawberries on each stick (approximately 4-6 pieces on each skewer). Brush kabobs with butter or margarine mixture, place on grill and cook, turning on all sides, until chicken is cooked through and strawberries are sizzling, approximately 8-10 minutes.

MIXED BERRIES WITH RASPBERRY VINAIGRETTE

Reggie Gordon

1 c. fresh STRAWBERRIES,
  halved
1 c. fresh blackberries
1 c. fresh blueberries

1 c. fresh raspberries
2 T. raspberry vinegar
2 T. vegetable oil

Combine strawberries, blackberries, blueberries, and raspberries, in a medium bowl, and toss gently. Combine berry juice, vinegar, and oil; stir well. Pour over berries; toss gently. Cover and chill at least 1 hour. Yield: 8 servings.

STRAWBERRY STUFF

Reggie Gordon

1 box frozen STRAWBERRIES
1 lg. Cool Whip
1 lg. can pineapple, drained

1 lg. bag miniature
  marshmallows

Stir ingredients together. Spread in 9 x 13-inch dish, refrigerate overnight. Serve with pound or nut cake.

STRAWBERRY BAVARIAN

Reggie Gordon

16 oz. frozen STRAWBERRIES, thawed
1/4 c. cold milk
2 env. unflavored gelatin
1/4 c. sugar

2 egg yolks
Red food coloring, opt.
2 c. whipping cream
1 c. crushed ice, drained

Drain strawberries, reserving 1/2 cup juice. Bring juice to a boil in a small saucepan. Combine milk, gelatin and hot juice in container of electric blender; blend about 1 minute. When gelatin is dissolved, add sugar, strawberries, egg yolks, and food coloring, if desired; continue blending until ice is liquified. Pour at once into serving dishes; let set 5-10 minutes before serving. Yield: 6-8 servings.

DEEP FRIED STRAWBERRIES

FSGA Women's Committee

24 lg. STRAWBERRIES
1 c. pancake mix

1/2 c. plus 2 T. milk
Vegetable oil

Sherry Sauce:

1 c. sifted powdered sugar
1/3 c. water

1 T. plus 3/4 tsp. cornstarch
1/4 c. sherry

Combine pancake mix and milk, stirring well. Dip strawberries in batter, and deep fry in hot oil (375°) until golden brown. Drain on paper towels. Serve strawberries immediately with sherry sauce. Combine sugar and water in a small saucepan; bring to a boil. Combine cornstarch and sherry, stirring until cornstarch dissolves. Gradually stir cornstarch mixture into hot mixture; cook over medium heat, stirring constantly, until sauce is smooth and thickened.

STRAWBERRY SAUCE WITH DUMPLINGS

Reggie Gordon

2 (16-oz.) pkgs. frozen whole STRAWBERRIES, thawed
1 c. water
2 T. sugar
2 T. butter
1/8 tsp. salt
1 c. all-purpose flour

1 1/2 tsp. baking powder
Dash of salt
1/4 c. sugar
2 T. butter
1/3 c. milk
1/2 tsp. vanilla extract
Ice cream, opt.

Combine strawberries, water, sugar, butter, salt in a saucepan; bring to a boil. Combine flour, baking powder, dash of salt, and 1/4 cup sugar; cut in 2 tablespoons butter until mixture resembles coarse meal. Stir in milk and vanilla; mix well. Drop mixture by teaspoonfuls into boiling

(continued)

34491B-00

strawberry mixture; cook uncovered 5 minutes. Cover, reduce heat, and simmer 15 minutes. Serve over ice cream, if desired. Yield: 8 servings.

STRAWBERRY PANCAKES

FSGA Women's Committee

½ c. puréed STRAWBERRIES   1 T. sugar
Favorite pancake recipe   Pinch of cinnamon

Prepare favorite pancake recipe. Add ½ cup puréed strawberries, 1 tablespoon sugar and a pinch of cinnamon. Blend well. Cook on hot greased griddle, turning when bubbles appear on pancake.

STRAWBERRY FRUIT LEATHER

FSGA Women's Committee

8 c. strawberries that have been   1 c. sugar
put through a blender   ¼ c. lemon juice

Put Saran Wrap on a cookie sheet and spread the strawberry mixture thin and evenly on the Saran Wrap. Place cookie sheet on top rack in the oven at 150°. Leave oven door open. This process takes several hours. An electric fruit dryer may be used or the cookie sheet may be set in the sun for several hours. Strawberries are dry when you can tear it like leather. Roll strawberries up still on same Saran Wrap and store in a tightly capped jar.

Recipe Favorites

Recipe Favorites

34491B-00

Berry Delightful Decorating

Strawberry Holiday Tree, page 117

Creative Decorating Uses
and Gift Ideas with
Florida Strawberries

BERRY DELIGHTFUL DECORATING

TIERS OF BERRIES

FSGA Women's Committee

Fresh Florida STRAWBERRIES
  with stems
Tiered plates, plate topped with
  pedestal plate, or stacks of
  plates using glasses to
  separate and hold

Greenery and/or wreaths

Fill the plates with strawberries, and garnish with greenery, fresh or artificial wreaths, to fill up empty spaces. Add candles and bows.

BERRY HOUSE

FSGA Women's Committee

Fresh Florida STRAWBERRIES
Styrofoam: a flat rectangular
  base and several flat sheets
  depending on theme.
For the church, you will need
  Styrofoam shapes to create the
  steeple.

Colored foil, example: use white
  for church, red for school
  house
Toothpicks

Place the flat Styrofoam base on a serving tray. Cover Styrofoam pieces with foil. You can use a glue gun to secure foil. Create the shape of the house with Styrofoam pieces. Use toothpicks to secure Styrofoam. Cover Styrofoam in toothpicks. Place the strawberries on the sides, through toothpicks. Do not put toothpicks through the green cap. Strawberry should point downward on the roof. For a church, dust the strawberries with powdered sugar, or dip them in white chocolate.

CORNUCOPIA OF BERRIES

FSGA Women's Committee

Fresh STRAWBERRIES
Rattan, china, crystal, wire or
  metal cornucopia (craft stores
  carry these)
For an edible cornucopia:
  rattan, wire or metal
  cornucopia

Foil
Pie, cookie or bread dough
Ribbon

For edible cornucopia, wrap the cornucopia with foil. Prepare dough. Roll into large and long strips of rope. Begin at opening and wrap dough rope around cornucopia until it reaches the tip. Secure with toothpicks,

(continued)

so dough will not slide. If you are using bread dough, allow it to rise before placing on cornucopia. Lay on cookie sheet and bake at the recommended oven temperature for the recipe you are using. When baked, let cool. Decorate with ribbons and bows. Fill with fresh strawberries.

BASKET-O-BERRIES

FSGA Women's Committee

**4 c. Florida STRAWBERRIES,
  washed and dried
Decorative basket**

**½ styrofoam ball
Toothpicks
Ribbon**

Place ½ styrofoam ball, dome side up, into the top of a basket. Insert toothpicks. Place whole berries with stems on toothpicks. Top the basket with a bow. Makes a great Valentine's Day gift.

BERRY BOX

FSGA Women's Committee

**Fresh Florida STRAWBERRIES
  with stems
Containers: boxes, buckets or
  crates**

Paper or straw

Enhance party tables with simple and unusual centerpieces made with fresh Florida strawberries. Fill containers with paper or straw. You do not want to stack the berries too deep, they will bruise. Cover containers with green cloth, doilies, straw or greenery. For a Christmas decoration cover boxes in wrapping paper and bows. Fill with strawberries.

STRAWBERRY CONE

FSGA Women's Committee

**Fresh Florida Strawberries with
  stems
Wooden cone, 10 inches tall, 6
  inch bottom, diameter to 2
  inches, a top studded with
  nails**

**Tree leaves
Powdered sugar**

Adorn plate with tree leaves. Place berries on nails. Dust with powdered sugar to give the illusion of snow.

116

EDIBLE STRAWBERRY BOUQUET

FSGA Women's Committee

4 pt. Florida STRAWBERRIES
  with stems, washed and dried
  well
Long, green florist picks

Long, gift box
Green tissue, or
Clear vase, greenery and bow

Layer gift box with green tissue. Place strawberries on picks. Arrange strawberry picks in gift basket or raise like a floral bouquet. Decorate with greenery and bows.

STRAWBERRY HOLIDAY TREE

FSGA Women's Committee

Fresh Florida STRAWBERRIES
  with green caps
Dinner plate
Greenery and foil candies
Wreath or pine boughs

Ribbon
Green foil
12-inch styrofoam cone
Long toothpicks

Surround plate with greenery and/or wreath. Cover Styrofoam cone with green foil. Place the large end of the cone on the plate. Stick one end of toothpick into the side of strawberries, and other side of toothpick into the styrofoam cone. Cover cone with strawberries. Fill in any hole or spaces with greenery, or candy. Keep a fresh supply of strawberries nearby to replenish the tree.

Recipe Favorites

Recipe Favorites

34491B-00

INDEX OF RECIPES

CAKES & COOKIES

WINTER WARMERS

COLD TREATS

INTERESTING & UNIQUE

BERRY DELIGHTFUL
DECORATING

How to Order

Get your additional copies of this cookbook by returning an order form and your check or money order to:

Florida Strawberry Growers Association
P.O. Drawer 2550
Plant City, FL 33564
(813) 752-6822

Please send me _____ copies of the **Simply Florida... Strawberries** cookbook at **$12.50** per copy and **$3.00** for shipping and handling per book. Enclosed is my check or money order for $_____.

Mail Books To:

Name _____

Address _____

City _____ State _____ Zip _____

✂ ---

Please send me _____ copies of the **Simply Florida... Strawberries** cookbook at **$12.50** per copy and **$3.00** for shipping and handling per book. Enclosed is my check or money order for $_____.

Mail Books To:

Name _____

Address _____

City _____ State _____ Zip _____

34491 j

PANTRY BASICS

A WELL-STOCKED PANTRY provides all the makings for a good meal. With the right ingredients, you can quickly create a variety of satisfying, delicious meals for family or guests. Keeping these items in stock also means avoiding extra trips to the grocery store, saving you time and money. Although everyone's pantry is different, there are basic items you should always have. Add other items according to your family's needs. For example, while some families consider chips, cereals and snacks as must-haves, others can't be without feta cheese and imported olives. Use these basic pantry suggestions as a handy reference list when creating your grocery list. Don't forget refrigerated items like milk, eggs, cheese and butter.

STAPLES

Baker's chocolate
Baking powder
Baking soda
Barbeque sauce
Bread crumbs (plain or seasoned)
Chocolate chips
Cocoa powder
Cornmeal
Cornstarch
Crackers
Flour
Honey
Ketchup
Lemon juice
Mayonnaise or salad dressing
Non-stick cooking spray
Nuts (almonds, pecans, walnuts)
Oatmeal
Oil (olive, vegetable)
Pancake baking mix
Pancake syrup
Peanut butter
Shortening
Sugar (granulated, brown, powdered)
Vinegar

PACKAGED/CANNED FOODS

Beans (canned, dry)
Broth (beef, chicken)
Cake mixes with frosting
Canned diced tomatoes
Canned fruit
Canned mushrooms
Canned soup
Canned tomato paste & sauce
Canned tuna & chicken
Cereal
Dried soup mix
Gelatin (flavored or plain)
Gravies
Jarred Salsa
Milk (evaporated, sweetened condensed)
Non-fat dry milk
Pastas
Rice (brown, white)
Spaghetti sauce

SPICES/SEASONINGS

Basil
Bay leaves
Black pepper
Boullion cubes (beef, chicken)
Chives
Chili powder
Cinnamon
Mustard (dried, prepared)
Garlic powder or salt
Ginger
Nutmeg
Onion powder or salt
Oregano
Paprika
Parsley
Rosemary
Sage
Salt
Soy sauce
Tarragon
Thyme
Vanilla
Worcestershire sauce
Yeast

HERBS & SPICES

DRIED VS. FRESH. While dried herbs are convenient, they don't generally have the same purity of flavor as fresh herbs. Ensure dried herbs are still fresh by checking if they are green and not faded. Crush a few leaves to see if the aroma is still strong. Always store them in an air-tight container away from light and heat.

BASIL
Sweet, warm flavor with an aromatic odor. Use whole or ground. Good with lamb, fish, roast, stews, beef, vegetables, dressing and omelets.

BAY LEAVES
Pungent flavor. Use whole leaf but remove before serving. Good in vegetable dishes, seafood, stews and pickles.

CARAWAY
Spicy taste and aromatic smell. Use in cakes, breads, soups, cheese and sauerkraut.

CELERY SEED
Strong taste which resembles the vegetable. Can be used sparingly in pickles and chutney, meat and fish dishes, salads, bread, marinades, dressings and dips.

CHIVES
Sweet, mild flavor like that of onion. Excellent in salads, fish, soups and potatoes.

CILANTRO
Use fresh. Excellent in salads, fish, chicken, rice, beans and Mexican dishes.

CINNAMON
Sweet, pungent flavor. Widely used in many sweet baked goods, chocolate dishes, cheesecakes, pickles, chutneys and hot drinks.

CORIANDER
Mild, sweet, orangy flavor and available whole or ground. Common in curry powders and pickling spice and also used in chutney, meat dishes, casseroles, Greek-style dishes, apple pies and baked goods.

CURRY POWDER
Spices are combined to proper proportions to give a distinct flavor to meat, poultry, fish and vegetables.

DILL
Both seeds and leaves are flavorful. Leaves may be used as a garnish or cooked with fish, soup, dressings, potatoes and beans. Leaves or the whole plant may be used to flavor pickles.

FENNEL
Sweet, hot flavor. Both seeds and leaves are used. Use in small quantities in pies and baked goods. Leaves can be boiled with fish.

DILL
Seeds

HERBS & SPICES

GINGER
A pungent root, this aromatic spice is sold fresh, dried or ground. Use in pickles, preserves, cakes, cookies, soups and meat dishes.

MARJORAM
May be used both dried or green. Use to flavor fish, poultry, omelets, lamb, stew, stuffing and tomato juice.

MINT
Aromatic with a cool flavor. Excellent in beverages, fish, lamb, cheese, soup, peas, carrots and fruit desserts.

NUTMEG
Whole or ground. Used in chicken and cream soups, cheese dishes, fish cakes, and with chicken and veal. Excellent in custards, milk puddings, pies and cakes.

OREGANO
Strong, aromatic odor. Use whole or ground in tomato juice, fish, eggs, pizza, omelets, chili, stew, gravy, poultry and vegetables.

PAPRIKA
A bright red pepper, this spice is used in meat, vegetables and soups or as a garnish for potatoes, salads or eggs.

PARSLEY
Best when used fresh, but can be used dried as a garnish or as a seasoning. Try in fish, omelets, soup, meat, stuffing and mixed greens.

ROSEMARY
Very aromatic. Can be used fresh or dried. Season fish, stuffing, beef, lamb, poultry, onions, eggs, bread and potatoes. Great in dressings.

SAFFRON
Aromatic, slightly bitter taste. Only a pinch needed to flavor and color dishes such as bouillabaisse, chicken soup, rice, paella, fish sauces, buns and cakes. Very expensive, so where a touch of color is needed, use turmeric instead, but the flavor will not be the same.

SAGE
Use fresh or dried. The flowers are sometimes used in salads. May be used in tomato juice, fish, omelets, beef, poultry, stuffing, cheese spreads and breads.

TARRAGON
Leaves have a pungent, hot taste. Use to flavor sauces, salads, fish, poultry, tomatoes, eggs, green beans, carrots and dressings.

THYME
Sprinkle leaves on fish or poultry before broiling or baking. Throw a few sprigs directly on coals shortly before meat is finished grilling.

TURMERIC
Aromatic, slightly bitter flavor. Should be used sparingly in curry powder and relishes and to color cakes and rice dishes.

Use 3 times more fresh herbs if substituting fresh for dried.

BAKING BREADS

HINTS FOR BAKING BREADS

• Kneading dough for 30 seconds after mixing improves the texture of baking powder biscuits.

• Instead of shortening, use cooking or salad oil in waffles and hot cakes.

• When bread is baking, a small dish of water in the oven will help keep the crust from hardening.

• Dip a spoon in hot water to measure shortening, butter, etc., and the fat will slip out more easily.

• Small amounts of leftover corn may be added to pancake batter for variety.

• To make bread crumbs, use the fine cutter of a food grinder and tie a large paper bag over the spout in order to prevent flying crumbs.

• When you are doing any sort of baking, you get better results if you remember to preheat your cookie sheet, muffin tins or cake pans.

3 RULES FOR USE OF LEAVENING AGENTS

1. In simple flour mixtures, use 2 teaspoons baking powder to leaven 1 cup flour. Reduce this amount 1/2 teaspoon for each egg used.

2. To 1 teaspoon soda, use 2 1/4 teaspoons cream of tartar, 2 cups freshly soured milk or 1 cup molasses.

3. To substitute soda and an acid for baking powder, divide the amount of baking powder by 4. Take that as your measure and add acid according to rule 2.

PROPORTIONS OF BAKING POWDER TO FLOUR

biscuits ....to 1 cup flour use 1 1/4 tsp. baking powder
cake with oil ....to 1 cup flour use 1 tsp. baking powder
muffins ....to 1 cup flour use 1 1/2 tsp. baking powder
popovers ....to 1 cup flour use 1 1/4 tsp. baking powder
waffles ....to 1 cup flour use 1 1/4 tsp. baking powder

PROPORTIONS OF LIQUID TO FLOUR

pour batter ....to 1 cup liquid use 1 cup flour
drop batter ....to 1 cup liquid use 2 to 2 1/2 cups flour
soft dough ....to 1 cup liquid use 3 to 3 1/2 cups flour
stiff dough ....to 1 cup liquid use 4 cups flour

TIME & TEMPERATURE CHART

Breads	Minutes	Temperature
biscuits	12 - 15	400° - 450°
cornbread	25 - 30	400° - 425°
gingerbread	40 - 50	350° - 370°
loaf	50 - 60	350° - 400°
nut bread	50 - 75	350°
popovers	30 - 40	425° - 450°
rolls	20 - 30	400° - 450°

BAKING DESSERTS

PERFECT COOKIES

Cookie dough that must be rolled is much easier to handle after it has been refrigerated for 10 to 30 minutes. This keeps the dough from sticking, even though it may be soft. If not done, the soft dough may require more flour and too much flour makes cookies hard and brittle. Place on a floured board only as much dough as can be easily managed. Flour the rolling pin slightly and roll lightly to desired thickness. Cut shapes close together and add trimmings to dough that needs to be rolled. Place pans or sheets in upper third of oven. Watch cookies carefully while baking in order to avoid burned edges. When sprinkling sugar on cookies, try putting it into a salt shaker in order to save time.

PERFECT PIES

• Pie crust will be better and easier to make if all the ingredients are cool.

• The lower crust should be placed in the pan so that it covers the surface smoothly. Air pockets beneath the surface will push the crust out of shape while baking.

• Folding the top crust over the lower crust before crimping will keep juices in the pie.

• When making custard pie, bake at a high temperature for about 10 minutes to prevent a soggy crust. Then finish baking at a low temperature.

• When making cream pie, sprinkle crust with powdered sugar in order to prevent it from becoming soggy.

PERFECT CAKES

• Fill cake pans two-thirds full and spread batter into corners and sides, leaving a slight hollow in the center.

• Cake is done when it shrinks from the sides of the pan or if it springs back when touched lightly with the finger.

• After removing a cake from the oven, place it on a rack for about 5 minutes. Then, the sides should be loosened and the cake turned out on a rack in order to finish cooling.

• Do not frost cakes until thoroughly cool.

• Icing will remain where you put it if you sprinkle cake with powdered sugar first.

TIME & TEMPERATURE CHART

Dessert	Time	Temperature
butter cake, layer	20-40 min.	380° - 400°
butter cake, loaf	40-60 min.	360° - 400°
cake, angel	50-60 min.	300° - 360°
cake, fruit	3-4 hrs.	275° - 325°
cake, sponge	40-60 min.	300° - 350°
cookies, molasses	18-20 min.	350° - 375°
cookies, thin	10-12 min.	380° - 390°
cream puffs	45-60 min.	300° - 350°
meringue	40-60 min.	250° - 300°
pie crust	20-40 min.	400° - 500°

VEGETABLES & FRUITS

COOKING TIME TABLE

Vegetable	Cooking Method	Time
artichokes	boiled	40 min.
	steamed	45-60 min.
asparagus tips	boiled	10-15 min.
beans, lima	boiled	20-40 min.
	steamed	60 min.
beans, string	boiled	15-35 min.
	steamed	60 min.
beets, old	boiled or steamed	1-2 hours.
beets, young with skin	boiled	30 min.
	steamed	60 min.
	baked	70-90 min.
broccoli, flowerets	boiled	5-10 min.
broccoli, stems	boiled	20-30 min.
brussels sprouts	boiled	20-30 min.
cabbage, chopped	boiled	10-20 min.
	steamed	25 min.
carrots, cut across	boiled	8-10 min.
	steamed	40 min.
cauliflower, flowerets	boiled	8-10 min.
cauliflower, stem down	boiled	20-30 min.
corn, green, tender	boiled	5-10 min.
	steamed	15 min.
	baked	20 min.
corn on the cob	boiled	8-10 min.
	steamed	15 min.
eggplant, whole	boiled	30 min.
	steamed	40 min.
	baked	45 min.
parsnips	boiled	25-40 min.
	steamed	60 min.
	baked	60-75 min.
peas, green	boiled or steamed	5-15 min.
potatoes	boiled	20-40 min.
	steamed	60 min.
	baked	45-60 min.
pumpkin or squash	boiled	20-40 min.
	steamed	45 min.
	baked	60 min.
tomatoes	boiled	5-15 min.
turnips	boiled	25-40 min.

DRYING TIME TABLE

Fruit	Sugar or Honey	Cooking Time
apricots	1/4 c. for each cup of fruit	about 40 min.
figs	1 T. for each cup of fruit	about 30 min.
peaches	1/4 c. for each cup of fruit	about 45 min.
prunes	2 T. for each cup of fruit	about 45 min.

VEGETABLES & FRUITS

BUYING FRESH VEGETABLES

Artichokes: Look for compact, tightly closed heads with green, clean-looking leaves. Avoid those with leaves that are brown or separated.

Asparagus: Stalks should be tender and firm; tips should be close and compact. Choose the stalks with very little white; they are more tender. Use asparagus soon because it toughens quickly.

Beans, Snap: Those with small seeds inside the pods are best. Avoid beans with dry-looking pods.

Broccoli, Brussels Sprouts and Cauliflower: Flower clusters on broccoli and cauliflower should be tight and close together. Brussels sprouts should be firm and compact. Smudgy, dirty spots may indicate pests or disease.

Cabbage and Head Lettuce: Choose heads that are heavy for their size. Avoid cabbage with worm holes and lettuce with discoloration or soft rot.

Cucumbers: Choose long, slender cucumbers for best quality. May be dark or medium green, but yellow ones are undesirable.

Mushrooms: Caps should be closed around the stems. Avoid black or brown gills.

Peas and Lima Beans: Select pods that are well-filled but not bulging. Avoid dried, spotted, yellow or limp pods.

BUYING FRESH FRUITS

Bananas: Skin should be free of bruises and black or brown spots. Purchase them slightly green and allow them to ripen at room temperature.

Berries: Select plump, solid berries with good color. Avoid stained containers which indicate wet or leaky berries. Berries with clinging caps, such as blackberries and raspberries, may be unripe. Strawberries without caps may be overripe.

Melons: In cantaloupes, thick, close netting on the rind indicates best quality. Cantaloupes are ripe when the stem scar is smooth and the space between the netting is yellow or yellow-green. They are best when fully ripe with fruity odor.

Honeydews are ripe when rind has creamy to yellowish color and velvety texture. Immature honeydews are whitish-green.

Ripe watermelons have some yellow color on one side. If melons are white or pale green on one side, they are not ripe.

Oranges, Grapefruit and Lemons: Choose those heavy for their size. Smoother, thinner skins usually indicate more juice. Most skin markings do not affect quality. Oranges with a slight greenish tinge may be just as ripe as fully colored ones. Light or greenish-yellow lemons are more tart than deep yellow ones. Avoid citrus fruits showing withered, sunken or soft areas.

NAPKIN FOLDING

FOR BEST RESULTS, use well-starched linen napkins if possible. For more complicated folds, 24-inch napkins work best. Practice the folds with newspapers. Children will have fun decorating the table once they learn these attractive folds!

SHIELD

Easy fold. Elegant with monogram in corner.

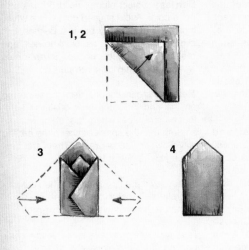

Instructions:
1. Fold into quarter size. If monogrammed, ornate corner should face down.
2. Turn up folded corner three-quarters.
3. Overlap right side and left side points.
4. Turn over; adjust sides so they are even, single point in center.
5. Place point up or down on plate, or left of plate.

ROSETTE

Elegant on plate.

Instructions:
1. Fold left and right edges to center, leaving ½" opening along center.
2. Pleat firmly from top edge to bottom edge. Sharpen edges with hot iron.
3. Pinch center together. If necessary, use small piece of pipe cleaner to secure and top with single flower.
4. Spread out rosette.

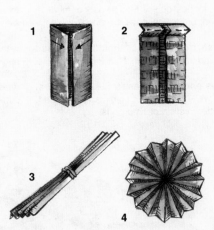

NAPKIN FOLDING

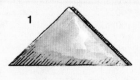

CANDLE

Easy to do; can be decorated.

Instructions:
1. Fold into triangle, point at top.
2. Turn lower edge up 1".
3. Turn over, folded edge down.
4. Roll tightly from left to right.
5. Tuck in corner. Stand upright.

FAN

Pretty in napkin ring or on plate.

Instructions:
1. Fold top and bottom edges to center.
2. Fold top and bottom edges to center a second time.
3. Pleat firmly from the left edge. Sharpen edges with hot iron.
4. Spread out fan. Balance flat folds of each side on table. Well-starched napkins will hold shape.

1, 2

3

4

LILY

Effective and pretty on table.

Instructions:
1. Fold napkin into quarters.
2. Fold into triangle, closed corner to open points.
3. Turn two points over to other side. (Two points are on either side of closed point.)
4. Pleat.
5. Place closed end in glass. Pull down two points on each side and shape.

1

2

3, 4

5

MEASUREMENTS & SUBSTITUTIONS

MEASUREMENTS

a pinch	1/8 teaspoon or less
3 teaspoons	1 tablespoon
4 tablespoons	1/4 cup
8 tablespoons	1/2 cup
12 tablespoons	3/4 cup
16 tablespoons	1 cup
2 cups	1 pint
4 cups	1 quart
4 quarts	1 gallon
8 quarts	1 peck
4 pecks	1 bushel
16 ounces	1 pound
32 ounces	1 quart
1 ounce liquid	2 tablespoons
8 ounces liquid	1 cup

Use standard measuring spoons and cups. All measurements are level.

C° TO F° CONVERSION

120° C	250° F
140° C	275° F
150° C	300° F
160° C	325° F
180° C	350° F
190° C	375° F
200° C	400° F
220° C	425° F
230° C	450° F

Temperature conversions are estimates.

SUBSTITUTIONS

Ingredient	Quantity	Substitute
baking powder	1 teaspoon	1/4 tsp. baking soda plus 1/2 tsp. cream of tartar
chocolate	1 square (1 oz.)	3 or 4 T. cocoa plus 1 T. butter
cornstarch	1 tablespoon	2 T. flour or 2 tsp. quick-cooking tapioca
cracker crumbs	3/4 cup	1 c. bread crumbs
dates	1 lb.	1 1/2 c. dates, pitted and cut
dry mustard	1 teaspoon	1 T. prepared mustard
flour, self-rising	1 cup	1 c. all-purpose flour, 1/2 tsp. salt, and 1 tsp. baking powder
herbs, fresh	1 tablespoon	1 tsp. dried herbs
ketchup or chili sauce	1 cup	1 c. tomato sauce plus 1/2 c. sugar and 2 T. vinegar (for use in cooking)
milk, sour	1 cup	1 T. lemon juice or vinegar plus sweet milk to make 1 c. (let stand 5 minutes)
whole	1 cup	1/2 c. evaporated milk plus 1/2 c. water
min. marshmallows	10	1 lg. marshmallow
onion, fresh	1 small	1 T. instant minced onion, rehydrated
sugar, brown	1/2 cup	2 T. molasses in 1/2 c. granulated sugar
powdered	1 cup	1 c. granulated sugar plus 1 tsp. cornstarch
tomato juice	1 cup	1/2 c. tomato sauce plus 1/2 c. water

When substituting cocoa for chocolate in cakes, the amount of flour must be reduced. Brown and white sugars usually can be interchanged.

EQUIVALENCY CHART

Food	Quantity	Yield
apple	1 medium	1 cup
banana, mashed	1 medium	1/3 cup
bread	1 1/2 slices	1 cup soft crumbs
bread	1 slice	1/4 cup fine, dry crumbs
butter	1 stick or 1/4 pound	1/2 cup
cheese, American, cubed	1 pound	2 2/3 cups
American, grated	1 pound	5 cups
cream cheese	3-ounce package	6 2/3 tablespoons
chocolate, bitter	1 square	1 ounce
cocoa	1 pound	4 cups
coconut	1 1/2 pound package	2 2/3 cups
coffee, ground	1 pound	5 cups
cornmeal	1 pound	3 cups
cornstarch	1 pound	3 cups
crackers, graham	14 squares	1 cup fine crumbs
saltine	28 crackers	1 cup fine crumbs
egg	4-5 whole	1 cup
whites	8-10	1 cup
yolks	10-12	1 cup
evaporated milk	1 cup	3 cups whipped
flour, cake, sifted	1 pound	4 1/2 cups
rye	1 pound	5 cups
white, sifted	1 pound	4 cups
white, unsifted	1 pound	3 3/4 cups
gelatin, flavored	3 1/4 ounces	1/2 cup
unflavored	1/4 ounce	1 tablespoon
lemon	1 medium	3 tablespoon juice
marshmallows	16	1/4 pound
noodles, cooked	8-ounce package	7 cups
uncooked	4 ounces (1 1/2 cups)	2-3 cups cooked
macaroni, cooked	8-ounce package	6 cups
macaroni, uncooked	4 ounces (1 1/4 cups)	2 1/4 cups cooked
spaghetti, uncooked	7 ounces	4 cups cooked
nuts, chopped	1/4 pound	1 cup
almonds	1 pound	3 1/2 cups
walnuts, broken	1 pound	3 cups
walnuts, unshelled	1 pound	1 1/2 to 1 3/4 cups
onion	1 medium	1/2 cup
orange	3-4 medium	1 cup juice
raisins	1 pound	3 1/2 cups
rice, brown	1 cup	4 cups cooked
converted	1 cup	3 1/2 cups cooked
regular	1 cup	3 cups cooked
wild	1 cup	4 cups cooked
sugar, brown	1 pound	2 1/2 cups
powdered	1 pound	3 1/2 cups
white	1 pound	2 cups
vanilla wafers	22	1 cup fine crumbs
zwieback, crumbled	4	1 cups

FOOD QUANTITIES

FOR LARGE SERVINGS

	25 Servings	50 Servings	100 Servings
Beverages:			
coffee	½ pound and 1 ½ gallons water	1 pound and 3 gallons water	2 pounds and 6 gallons water
lemonade	10-15 lemons and 1 ½ gallons water	20-30 lemons and 3 gallons water	40-60 lemons and 6 gallons water
tea	1/12 pound and 1 ½ gallons water	1/6 pound and 3 gallons water	1/3 pound and 6 gallons water
Desserts:			
layered cake	1 12" cake	3 10" cakes	6 10" cakes
sheet cake	1 10" x 12" cake	1 12" x 20" cake	2 12" x 20" cakes
watermelon	37 ½ pounds	75 pounds	150 pounds
whipping cream	¾ pint	1 ½ to 2 pints	3-4 pints
Ice cream:			
brick	3 ¼ quarts	6 ½ quarts	13 quarts
bulk	2 ¼ quarts	4 ½ quarts or 1 ¼ gallons	9 quarts or 2 ½ gallons
Meat, poultry or fish:			
fish	13 pounds	25 pounds	50 pounds
fish, fillets or steak	7 ½ pounds	15 pounds	30 pounds
hamburger	9 pounds	18 pounds	35 pounds
turkey or chicken	13 pounds	25 to 35 pounds	50 to 75 pounds
wieners (beef)	6 ½ pounds	13 pounds	25 pounds
Salads, casseroles:			
baked beans	¾ gallon	1 ¼ gallons	2 ½ gallons
jello salad	¾ gallon	1 ¼ gallons	2 ½ gallons
potato salad	4 ¼ quarts	2 ¼ gallons	4 ½ gallons
scalloped potatoes	4 ½ quarts or 1 12" x 20" pan	9 quarts or 2 ¼ gallons	18 quarts 4 ½ gallons
spaghetti	1 ¼ gallons	2 ½ gallons	5 gallons
Sandwiches:			
bread	50 slices or 3 1-pound loaves	100 slices or 6 1-pound loaves	200 slices or 12 1-pound loaves
butter	½ pound	1 pound	2 pounds
lettuce	1 ½ heads	3 heads	6 heads
mayonnaise	1 cup	2 cups	4 cups
mixed filling			
meat, eggs, fish	1 ½ quarts	3 quarts	6 quarts
jam, jelly	1 quart	2 quarts	4 quarts

QUICK FIXES

PRACTICALLY EVERYONE has experienced that dreadful moment in the kitchen when a recipe failed and dinner guests have arrived. Perhaps a failed timer, distraction or a missing or mismeasured ingredient is to blame. These handy tips can save the day!

Acidic foods – Sometimes a tomato-based sauce will become too acidic. Add baking soda, one teaspoon at a time, to the sauce. Use sugar as a sweeter alternative.

Burnt food on pots and pans – Allow the pan to cool on its own. Remove as much of the food as possible. Fill with hot water and add a capful of liquid fabric softener to the pot; let it stand for a few hours. You'll have an easier time removing the burnt food.

Chocolate seizes – Chocolate can seize (turn course and grainy) when it comes into contact with water. Place seized chocolate in a metal bowl over a large saucepan with an inch of simmering water in it. Over medium heat, slowly whisk in warm heavy cream. Use 1/4 cup cream to 4 ounces of chocolate. The chocolate will melt and become smooth.

Forgot to thaw whipped topping – Thaw in microwave for 1 minute on the defrost setting. Stir to blend well. Do not over thaw!

Hands smell like garlic or onion – Rinse hands under cold water while rubbing them with a large stainless steel spoon.

Hard brown sugar – Place in a paper bag and microwave for a few seconds, or place hard chunks in a food processor.

Jello too hard – Heat on a low microwave power setting for a very short time.

Lumpy gravy or sauce – Use a blender, food processor or simply strain.

No tomato juice – Mix 1/2 cup ketchup with 1/2 cup water.

Out of honey – Substitute 1 1/4 cups sugar dissolved in 1 cup water.

Overcooked sweet potatoes or carrots – Softened sweet potatoes and carrots make a wonderful soufflé with the addition of eggs and sugar. Consult your favorite cookbook for a good soufflé recipe. Overcooked sweet potatoes can also be used as pie filling.

Sandwich bread is stale – Toast or microwave bread briefly. Otherwise, turn it into breadcrumbs. Bread exposed to light and heat will hasten its demise, so consider using a bread box.

Soup, sauce, gravy too thin – Add 1 tablespoon of flour to hot soup, sauce or gravy. Whisk well (to avoid lumps) while the mixture is boiling. Repeat if necessary.

Sticky rice – Rinse rice with warm water.

Stew or soup is greasy – Refrigerate and remove grease once it congeals. Another trick is to lay cold lettuce leaves over the hot stew for about 10 seconds and then remove. Repeat as necessary.

Too salty – Add a little sugar and vinegar. For soups or sauces, add a raw peeled potato.

Too sweet – Add a little vinegar or lemon juice.

Undercooked cakes and cookies – Serve over vanilla ice cream. You can also layer pieces of cake or cookies with whipped cream and fresh fruit to form a dessert parfait. Crumbled cookies also make an excellent ice cream or cream pie topping.

COUNTING CALORIES

BEVERAGES

apple juice, 6 oz.	90
coffee (black)	0
cola, 12 oz.	115
cranberry juice, 6 oz.	115
ginger ale, 12 oz.	115
grape juice, (prepared from frozen concentrate), 6 oz.	142
lemonade, (prepared from frozen concentrate), 6 oz.	85
milk, protein fortified, 1 c.	105
skim, 1 c.	90
whole, 1 c.	160
orange juice, 6 oz.	85
pineapple juice, unsweetened, 6 oz.	95
root beer, 12 oz.	150
tonic (quinine water) 12 oz.	132

BREADS

cornbread, 1 sm. square	130
dumplings, 1 med.	70
French toast, 1 slice	135
melba toast, 1 slice	25
muffins, blueberry, 1 muffin	110
bran, 1 muffin	106
corn, 1 muffin	125
English, 1 muffin	280
pancakes, 1 (4-in.)	60
pumpernickel, 1 slice	75
rye, 1 slice	60
waffle, 1	216
white, 1 slice	60-70
whole wheat, 1 slice	55-65

CEREALS

cornflakes, 1 c.	105
cream of wheat, 1 c.	120
oatmeal, 1 c.	148
rice flakes, 1 c.	105
shredded wheat, 1 biscuit	100
sugar krisps, 3/4 c.	110

CRACKERS

graham, 1 cracker	15-30
rye crisp, 1 cracker	35
saltine, 1 cracker	17-20
wheat thins, 1 cracker	9

DAIRY PRODUCTS

butter or margarine, 1 T.	100
cheese, American, 1 oz.	100
camembert, 1 oz.	85
cheddar, 1 oz.	115
cottage cheese, 1 oz.	30
mozzarella, 1 oz.	90
parmesan, 1 oz.	130
ricotta, 1 oz.	50
roquefort, 1 oz.	105
Swiss, 1 oz.	105
cream, light, 1 T.	30
heavy, 1 T.	55
sour, 1 T.	45
hot chocolate, with milk, 1 c.	277
milk chocolate, 1 oz.	145-155
yogurt	
made w/ whole milk, 1 c.	150-165
made w/ skimmed milk, 1 c.	125

EGGS

fried, 1 lg.	100
poached or boiled, 1 lg.	75-80
scrambled or in omelet, 1 lg.	110-130

FISH AND SEAFOOD

bass, 4 oz.	105
salmon, broiled or baked, 3 oz.	155
sardines, canned in oil, 3 oz.	170
trout, fried, 3 1/2 oz.	220
tuna, in oil, 3 oz.	170
in water, 3 oz.	110

COUNTING CALORIES

FRUITS

apple, 1 med.	80-100
applesauce, sweetened, 1/2 c.	90-115
unsweetened, 1/2 c.	50
banana, 1 med.	85
blueberries, 1/2 c.	45
cantaloupe, 1/2 c.	24
cherries (pitted), raw, 1/2 c.	40
grapefruit, 1/2 med.	55
grapes, 1/2 c.	35-55
honeydew, 1/2 c.	55
mango, 1 med.	90
orange, 1 med.	65-75
peach, 1 med.	35
pear, 1 med.	60-100
pineapple, fresh, 1/2 c.	40
canned in syrup, 1/2 c.	95
plum, 1 med.	30
strawberries, fresh, 1/2 c.	30
frozen and sweetened, 1/2 c.	120-140
tangerine, 1 lg.	39
watermelon, 1/2 c.	42

MEAT AND POULTRY

beef, ground (lean), 3 oz.	185
roast, 3 oz.	185
chicken, broiled, 3 oz.	115
lamb chop (lean), 3 oz.	175-200
steak, sirloin, 3 oz.	175
tenderloin, 3 oz.	174
top round, 3 oz.	162
turkey, dark meat, 3 oz.	175
white meat, 3 oz.	150
veal, cutlet, 3 oz.	156
roast, 3 oz.	76

NUTS

almonds, 2 T.	105
cashews, 2 T.	100
peanuts, 2 T.	105
peanut butter, 1 T.	95
pecans, 2 T.	95
pistachios, 2 T.	92
walnuts, 2 T.	80

PASTA

macaroni or spaghetti, cooked, 3/4 c.	115

SALAD DRESSINGS

blue cheese, 1 T.	70
French, 1 T.	65
Italian, 1 T.	80
mayonnaise, 1 T.	100
olive oil, 1 T.	124
Russian, 1 T.	70
salad oil, 1 T.	120

SOUPS

bean, 1 c.	130-180
beef noodle, 1 c.	70
bouillon and consomme, 1 c.	30
chicken noodle, 1 c.	65
chicken with rice, 1 c.	50
minestrone, 1 c.	80-150
split pea, 1 c.	145-170
tomato with milk, 1 c.	170
vegetable, 1 c.	80-100

VEGETABLES

asparagus, 1 c.	35
broccoli, cooked, 1/2 c.	25
cabbage, cooked, 1/2 c.	15-20
carrots, cooked, 1/2 c.	25-30
cauliflower, 1/2 c.	10-15
corn (kernels), 1/2 c.	70
green beans, 1 c.	30
lettuce, shredded, 1/2 c.	5
mushrooms, canned, 1/2 c.	20
onions, cooked, 1/2 c.	30
peas, cooked, 1/2 c.	60
potato, baked, 1 med.	90
chips, 8-10	100
mashed, w/milk & butter, 1 c.	200-300
spinach, 1 c.	40
tomato, raw, 1 med.	25
cooked, 1/2 c.	30

COOKING TERMS

Au gratin: Topped with crumbs and/or cheese and browned in oven or under broiler.

Au jus: Served in its own juices.

Baste: To moisten foods during cooking with pan drippings or special sauce in order to add flavor and prevent drying.

Bisque: A thick cream soup.

Blanch: To immerse in rapidly boiling water and allow to cook slightly.

Cream: To soften a fat, especially butter, by beating it at room temperature. Butter and sugar are often creamed together, making a smooth, soft paste.

Crimp: To seal the edges of a two-crust pie either by pinching them at intervals with the fingers or by pressing them together with the tines of a fork.

Crudites: An assortment of raw vegetables (i.e. carrots, broccoli, celery, mushrooms) that is served as an hors d'oeuvre, often accompanied by a dip.

Degrease: To remove fat from the surface of stews, soups or stock. Usually cooled in the refrigerator so that fat hardens and is easily removed.

Dredge: To coat lightly with flour, cornmeal, etc.

Entree: The main course.

Fold: To incorporate a delicate substance, such as whipped cream or beaten egg whites, into another substance without releasing air bubbles. A spatula is used to gently bring part of the mixture from the bottom of the bowl to the top. The process is repeated, while slowly rotating the bowl, until the ingredients are thoroughly blended.

Glaze: To cover with a glossy coating, such as a melted and somewhat diluted jelly for fruit desserts.

Julienne: To cut or slice vegetables, fruits or cheeses into match-shaped slivers.

Marinate: To allow food to stand in a liquid in order to tenderize or to add flavor.

Meuniére: Dredged with flour and sautéed in butter.

Mince: To chop food into very small pieces.

Parboil: To boil until partially cooked; to blanch. Usually final cooking in a seasoned sauce follows this procedure.

Pare: To remove the outermost skin of a fruit or vegetable.

Poach: To cook gently in hot liquid kept just below the boiling point.

Purée: To mash foods by hand by rubbing through a sieve or food mill, or by whirling in a blender or food processor until perfectly smooth.

Refresh: To run cold water over food that has been parboiled in order to stop the cooking process quickly.

Sauté: To cook and/or brown food in a small quantity of hot shortening.

Scald: To heat to just below the boiling point, when tiny bubbles appear at the edge of the saucepan.

Simmer: To cook in liquid just below the boiling point. The surface of the liquid should be barely moving, broken from time to time by slowly rising bubbles.

Steep: To let food stand in hot liquid in order to extract or to enhance flavor, like tea in hot water or poached fruit in syrup.

Toss: To combine ingredients with a repeated lifting motion.

Whip: To beat rapidly in order to incorporate air and produce expansion, as in heavy cream or egg whites.

Publish Your Own Cookbook

Morris Press Cookbooks has all the right ingredients to make a really great cookbook. Your group can raise $500 – $50,000 or create a cookbook as a lasting keepsake, preserving favorite family recipes.

You supply the recipes & we'll do the rest!™

3 ways to order our **FREE** Cookbook Kit:

- Call us at **800-445-6621, ext. CB**.
- Visit our web site at **www.morriscookbooks.com**.
- Complete and mail the **postage-paid reply card** below.